HUNTING
YOU'VE GOT TO BE KIDDING!

KEVIN DETTLER

Hunting: You've Got to Be Kidding!

This book is written to provide information and motivation to readers. Its purpose is not to render any type of psychological, legal, or professional advice of any kind. The content is the sole opinion and expression of the author, and not necessarily that of the publisher.

Printed in the United States of America.

ISBN   978-1-951913-43-4   (Paperback)
ISBN   978-1-951913-44-1   (Digital)

Lettra Press books may be ordered through booksellers or by contacting:

Lettra Press LLC
30 N Gould St. Suite 4753
Sheridan, WY 82801
1 307-200-3414 | info@lettrapress.com
www.lettrapress.com

The book cover portrays a picture of Muncho Lake, British Columbia, taken by the author from a spot where very few people have ever seen.

CONTENTS

DEDICATION

I love my wife, Becky, dearly. She deserves considerably more praise than this forum will provide. I am thankful for Becky's personality. She is loving, entertaining, friendly, persevering, and more.

It takes a very special woman to be the wife of a big game hunter. Becky and I were married thirty-eight years ago. I knew then she was very special. Every marriage has its trials, but asking a wife to endure her husband's passion for big game hunting is ridiculous. This is especially true for me because I was gone anywhere from two weeks to a month every year. I really don't know how Becky stood for this, but I tell her every day how blessed I am to be married to her.

The words "football widow" has very little meaning as compared to the words "hunting widow." Our love has grown over the years, and it is now my turn to allow Becky to pursue her passion.

My Beautiful Wife

Becky is also a wonderful mother. As our kids were growing up, she never missed a school event, a ball game, a recital, or any opportunity to be involved in their lives. Our children have been her passion, but today that passion is multiplied to provide attention not only to our children but also to our extended family and our seven grandchildren. Becky does more for friends or relatives than anyone else I know. She is always there for whoever needs her. She is a good organizer of her time thus can spend the time necessary to help where needed. I am not an organized person. Becky has been my inspiration through the years to finish my projects, including the following pages.

One of her greatest gifts is the ability to forgive. As I left for each hunt, Becky was mad. Maybe the word "mad" is too strong, but she was certainly disappointed. The hunt was less of a problem than the fact I would be away from her and the kids. Thank God, she is blessed with her forgiving nature as I was always welcomed home.

Thank you for the eternal love!

ACKNOWLEDGMENTS

First, Becky thank you for the never-ending support as I muddled through the processes to put these words together. Thanks to our children, our daughter, Nicole, for all the picture work and feedback on my writing style, and our sons, Kiel and Brett, for the encouragement and the extra hours they worked to cover for me. Thanks also to my father and mother for the inspiration, love, and feedback as the chapters emerged from the word processor.

Second, I would like to thank my friends for listening to my ramblings each time I returned home from a hunting trip. It was probably a natural progression from those stories to this book. I was encouraged to write mostly to reduce the barrage of storytelling to those who were still listening. In reality, some of my friends heard my tales so often I am sure they could have also produced this book.

Hunting: You've Got to Be Kidding! contains a great number of people's names. They are all real people, and I absolutely consider them friends. I highly recommend them as outfitter, guide, pilot, cook, or whatever capacity they served in my hunting career.

Last, thanks to Brandon Bagley and his staff at AlphaGraphics printing store in Gilbert, Arizona, for all the support in operating Word 2010 and taking all my phone calls while I learned how to write and organize a book.

CHAPTER 1

Nanook

The temperature outside has warmed to a balmy -25 degrees Fahrenheit. Because it has warmed, there are seals everywhere I look. They lie next to their breathing holes in the Arctic sea ice, absorbing the little bit of warmth the day offers. I tell the young Inuit guide seated to my right, with whom I have hunted the last seventeen days and nights, we should break out our golf shorts and the suntan lotion. He laughs, but I am not sure he understands the humor I try to add to our conversation. The previous sixteen days, we enjoyed temperatures as low as -55 degrees Fahrenheit, without windchill. As each cold day passed, I kept saying "YOU'VE GOT TO BE KIDDING." The sky today is eerie with patchy fog at what appears to be one hundred feet above the sea ice and heavy clouds the color of chocolate swirl in all directions. Certainly a look I wouldn't have expected in the artic.

The wind earlier today caused another whiteout, but now at 2:00 p.m. on day 17 of this hunt, the wind has died to an almost bearable (pun intended) breeze of a few miles per hour. I have once again returned to my usual optimistic outlook. This optimism has been hard to retain lately as even earlier in the week, wind speeds produced whiteout conditions and forced us to stay for three straight days in the confines of our Arctic Hilton hotel. Our penthouse suite is a four-foot-high tent, with about six by eight feet dimensions. My young Inuit guide, his uncle John and I occupy it.

During this whiteout and the other, we are huddled in our sleeping bags. With the help of a little Coleman cookstove, we are able to get the temperature in the tent to a little above zero degrees. My fellow campers are much more comfortable than I am due to the fact they are almost a foot shorter than myself. I am only able to get to my knees without my head being scrunched into the tent roof, and this makes getting dressed and putting on heavy clothes and boots nearly impossible.

Last week, we spent the three days in a row confined to the tent (alias penthouse suite) as the wind blew in excess of 60 miles per hour. I really didn't want to eat or drink very much for those three days because imagine having to get dressed to go outside and use the outdoor bathroom with temperatures at more than -100 degrees Fahrenheit, including the windchill. I brought along four books to read, and during these three days, I read all of them, not once but twice. Two of them have a terribly boring story line, but I read them twice anyway. It is interesting to note that after this hunt Becky bought me a Kindle as a Christmas gift. At least passing the time could have been a little more bearable.

The penthouse suite, our home for 20 days

I'm not a patient person, and putting in these three days with my two Inuit guides, one of whom speak as much English as I speak Spanish (I know only a few words like cerveza and por favor) is frustrating. I am having a hard time keeping the little sanity I have left. I have asked myself quite a few times the following question:

"Who in their right mind would spend in excess of $45,000 to have the experience I am having?" The whiteout conditions have been a very real part of the camping trip I am currently enjoying. In fact, only thirteen of the seventeen days on this trip have been suitable to complete the task at hand.

Since the wind has subsided today, we once again hook our nine dogs to the wood sled that has been my ride for about fifteen hours per day for the thirteen of the days that were suitable for travel. As we have done before, we set out in search of very large tracks or a glimpse of an animal itself. We are some 40–100 miles from land and, at times, will be over 250 miles from the small Inuit village of Holman, Northwest Territories, Canada, where this hunt began.

Holman NWT, Canada One of America's farthest north villages

The hunt I am on is one of nearly forty big game hunts that I have endured and enjoyed over the last twenty years. After completing about a fourth of these hunts, I had a dream, as a hunter, to complete a collection of animals that would qualify me for the North American 29 award as Safari Club International (SCI) calls it. SCI is a worldwide organization with membership in excess of 200,000, consisting of hunters, outfitters, and associates. They protect hunting rights and provide funds and guidance to increase habitat for wild animals. The North American 29 award honors hunters who have legally hunted and taken twenty-nine different species of big game animals that call North America their home. The number of member hunters who have currently taken and officially registered the North American 29 with SCI is less than 120. I know you're thinking, YOU'VE GOT TO BE KIDDING. Absolutely true. So you can see it is an elite group of hunters to have received the award. This hunt I'm on, if I successfully take my polar bear or "Nanook" in the Inuit language, will give me my twenty-nine species.

I spent a great amount of time deciding to write this book. More than a few have encouraged me to stop procrastinating, tell my story, and follow the words of Larry the Cable Guy, "GET 'ER DONE." My reservations in writing these words were twofold. First, there are already thousands of books written in North America and elsewhere in the world about hunting, trophy hunting, and animal behavior. Second, life's incredible moments, whether they be humorous, sad, or something in between, are sometimes extremely hard to convert to words that will produce for the reader the same reaction as the person writing the story.

With this story, I hope that you will get a sense of the emotional roller coaster associated with the accomplishment of my hunting goals. Now I would be foolish to think that the hunters among you haven't gone through these same emotions. Hopefully, you can associate with my triumphs and trials and enjoy some of my "YOU'VE GOT TO BE KIDDING" moments that I share in the following pages.

This book of hunting contains no lengthy descriptions of animal habits, nor do I try to promote the best places to hunt or which rifle or bow you should use. You can get all that from books already written or internet searches. What this book does contain is my story of having a dream and finding the ways financially, physically, and spiritually to achieve it. Yes, you need to have a lot of financing or cash and be fit and trim for most hunts in North America, but most of all, you have to have a deep faith in God that anything is possible.

You will learn that for me to be successful at achieving the North American 29, three things had to happen simultaneously. These three things come after my faith in God. First, I needed to be in above-average physical condition as hunting for different species in North America tends to be some of the most demanding on the planet. Second, the time involved is incredible. I spent no less than an average of six weeks every year for almost twenty years hunting, researching, flying, driving to and from airports, delivering to my taxidermist, practicing shooting, packing and unpacking, picking up from my taxidermist, arranging the animals in the trophy room, rearranging the trophy room, developing thousands of pictures, and filling out the necessary paperwork for licenses and trip reports. Third, you need the ability to have or borrow the necessary funds to cover the incredibly high costs of hunting in North America. If a hunter started today with the goal of collecting the North American 29 and figuring at least a little luck, it would take in excess of $1 million to complete. I know you're thinking, YOU'VE GOT TO BE KIDDING, but this is a very real number. Therefore, to be successful, you need good health, money, and time simultaneously. You have no idea how God blessed me, and I was able to align these three in my life so my dream could become reality.

As to the financial side of my story, wealth can come in a variety of packages. Most would associate wealth with money. I am not now nor was I ever a financially wealthy man. But I have incredible wealth. I have been fortunate to have grown up with a complete loving family—Father Aelred, Mother Doreen, and five siblings, all of whom are still married to their first spouse. Oh, by the way, the six of us—myself, my three brothers, and my two sisters—were all born within six years, thus earning my parents their own "YOU'VE GOT TO BE KIDDING."

I married my wonderful wife of almost thirty-eight years, Becky, when I was twenty-five. We have three incredible children—Nicole, Kiel, and Brett—and seven grandchildren—Ethan, Connor, Mya, Lennon, Madison, Scarlett and Emerson. Together with the love of these people and the many friendships I enjoy, I have a wealth greater than any amount of money could buy. They are the reason I was able to spend so much time pursuing my dream.

I was born into a farming family and continue to farm to this day. My parents gave me my start in the farming business. They were my moral support always, including the rough financial times. My wife and children always supported my goals, running the farm in my absence, which enabled me to go hunting. They all drove farm equipment, whether it was planting or harvesting, and managed the help and finances while I was collecting my species of animals. In this and the following chapters, you will see how much I needed their help for my dream to become reality.

Back to the story in the Arctic. With each passing day, I have become impatient and want to get done. While we are jailed in our tent this morning of day 17 because of the whiteout conditions, I have even more reason to be frustrated, almost depressed. John, the head guide, who speaks very little English but has a wonderful sense of humor, is talking in native tongue to his village of Holman, at least 250 miles away. The radios are operable for sometimes a thousand miles because of the flatness of the sea ice. John, with the help of translation from my young guide, as a way of promoting even further my disappointed state of mind, proceeds to tell me of another hunter. It seems a hunter from Wisconsin had arrived yesterday in the village of Holman (four hundred Inuit inhabitants) on the weekly flight from Yellowknife, Northwest Territories. The next day, they suited him up in the caribou skins, which provide extra warmth for the hunter, and headed out onto the sea ice right near the village with the dog team. Polar bears can only be hunted from a dogsled as no motorized vehicles are allowed. Within hours, he has killed his polar bear, with a bow, no less, and is back in the village, enjoying the warmth of one of the two rooms in the hotel in the village. They keep these rooms open for sport hunters or someone traveling to Holman on business.

When I hear this story, all I can say is "YOU'VE GOT TO BE KIDDING." Am I mad? No. Okay, maybe a little. Am I frustrated after being out on the ice for seventeen days and still not taking my bear? Am I mad because even if I got my trophy today, I am faced with a three-day trip just to get back to Holman? Yes, I am. I have to be honest as this hunt has been an emotional challenge for me.

Let's fast-forward here in the story to my arrival back in Holman on day 20. Jim, the hunter from Wisconsin, is still there as once again, the plane from Yellowknife only comes once a week. He has one of two rooms at the Holman hotel. He is a very humble person, and I was thrilled to meet him. The conversation quickly went from how big his bear was to me lamenting about my long camping trip. I told him he had to be the luckiest person I had ever met. He looked at me, puzzled, and asked why I thought that. I said plainly anyone who comes to Holman and gets his bear on the first day has to be lucky. With that, he said quietly, "Well, you know, I was here last year and hunted for twenty days and didn't get a bear, so I had to return this year and spend another $45,000." I think you could have heard a pin drop. I really have never been so embarrassed. I asked myself how I could be so stupid and self-centered to think I was the only one who may have trouble hunting polar bears. I just shook my head, thought about my shortcomings, and whispered to myself, "YOU'VE GOT TO BE KIDDING."

Now on this, day 17, we have been out on the ice in the dogsled for about two hours and haven't cut a single bear track. I keep reminding myself that even though success seems far away, it only takes a short time for things to come together for a successful hunt. The day remains very calm with the eerie clouds still about a hundred feet above us. I have never experienced anything like it. It's not snowing, but it looks as though the sky could just dump snow on us at any time. I don't know the logistics of finding our way to the tent in thousands of square miles of ice in a blizzard, but I really am worried. This feeling isn't unusual as I have been worried for most of this hunt. I am a very optimistic person, but there are dangers here that could take your life. I don't like to be cold, and my Northern Outfitters clothing has done a good job of protecting me from the elements. However, while I have not exactly been cold, I've never really gotten warm either. The prospect of freezing to death is ever present in your thoughts in this landscape and the conditions we've experienced.

A few days ago, something happened that could have cost us our lives. It was day 10, and we had left the tent early. After a few hours, we stopped. John was off the sled, and I could see he was perplexed with something. I finally gathered, after grappling with his broken English, that he was looking at a crack in the sea ice. The crack was one inch wide, and I could not understand the concern John seemed to be haggling with. My idea is "Get in the sled and let's go as you can see, the ice is over six feet thick." Finally, I learned from John that if we crossed over, we may return later to a crack that had gone from one inch to a mile wide. Now I didn't like this at all and expressed my concerns. Evidently, the language barrier had something to do with what happened next because we crossed the crack and continued. I thought John understood my concerns about crossing over.

My ride for 20 days, it was pulled by the dogs

I really didn't enjoy the rest of the day as I was thinking of my obituary: an insane farmer from South Dakota died on the Arctic Ocean after ice crack became too wide and he could not return home.

Sure enough, while we were hunting during the day, that guy called Murphy was busy, and when we came back to the crack, it was too wide to cross. I said, "YOU'VE GOT TO BE KIDDING." John, once again the comedian, said, "Don't worry, we'll try a different place." Now I didn't know if he meant we were going one mile or two thousand miles. As we followed along our side of the ice crack, I suddenly realized it was almost dark. I was really worried because I didn't know how John would get us to the tent in the dark as we usually returned to our penthouse in the daylight.

Well, God was with us. We found a place only one feet wide and crossed over. It was dark by then. I have no idea how the Inuit navigate on a flat white topography with no landmarks and complete darkness, but we did arrive at the tent around midnight. At that point, I was ready to quit this hunt and return home, although with a little rest overnight, my optimism returned.

Back to day 17 and the hunt. John stops the sled to do some glassing. I have not been able to help him spot bears as my face freezes instantly when I take my face mask off to put my binoculars up to glass for bears. So I did the next best thing. I gave John my Zeiss binoculars and let him do the looking. The usual procedure is for John to climb on the pressure ridges and look for actual bears. He says he has had more success this way than following tracks. Hey, who am I to argue as I've seen eight bears so far in this hunt with John doing the glassing?

A pressure ridge is a twenty to (sometimes) thirty feet tall fold of ice pushed upward when the wind blows around huge pieces of sea ice. They crash together and form these structures that help provide a platform for us to look for bears. The seals keep airholes open in the pressure ridges to facilitate breathing. They also give birth to their young along the pressure ridges. The polar bears can smell the seals or their young up to fifteen miles away and are always traveling along the ridges, looking for their next meal.

Do you ever get that feeling that something strange is about to happen? Well, I got that feeling when I saw John climbing down off the ridge. His face is like leather, formed from years of exposure

9

to the cruel temperatures of the Arctic winter. It's hard to tell, but I think I see a trace of a smile on his face, if that's possible when one's face is frozen…This story continues later as I revert back to the start of my attempt to achieve the North American 29. The following chapters are arranged in chronological order from early to late to facilitate an understanding of the entire process.

John looking for bears from the pressure ridge

CHAPTER 2

North To Alaska

Wow, I am excited! I have just hung up the phone (yes, for you, young "uns," we actually had to hang it up on the wall) after visiting with my booking agent from the great state of Texas. It is November 1991, and I have just returned from a successful elk hunt in Colorado. Fred Romley's services, like all hunt booking agents, are free for the hunter. He earns his living by retaining 15 percent of the cost of the hunt when the hunter's money is sent to the outfitter who will be conducting the hunt. It really is a good program as most hunters do not have the time to research all the right places to hunt, and so they rely on help from agents like Fred.

He is a very good salesman, at least in my case, or maybe I'm an easy sell. You know both of these statements are probably right. Fred booked the elk hunt in Colorado for my brother Dave and me. He was also able to join us, and we had a great time. Although Fred is not a drinker, he didn't interfere with my brother and me partaking of the spirits offered at camp. Much like my young guide in chapter 1, Fred may have been unsure how to take some of the humor a couple of farm boys doled out after a few totties. We teased him that a good booking agent should have gotten his client a much bigger elk. The elk I got was actually a very nice six-point, and Fred couldn't figure out why we kept calling it little. He would have been thrilled if he had taken it. Anyway, this elk is the first on my North American 29 list, and the rest of that story happens in chapter 18.

Back to the phone call. Once again, I couldn't say no when Fred said he thought I should try Alaska and sheep hunting. I haven't been to Alaska, but I really have been thinking of something other than elk and deer hunting for some time. Isn't it funny how a person's life story evolves in a certain direction because of the people who become part of his life? My life changed forever after meeting Fred Romley. I may have eventually gone to Alaska and started sheep hunting, but then again, I may never have let my hunting career get past "elk fever."

Fred did the booking for an Alaskan outfitter named Don Trautman, who operated between the town of Deadhorse and the Brooks Range in Alaska. Don had a very good area to hunt and offered multiple species hunts, including Dall sheep, Alaskan moose, Alaskan caribou, grizzly bear, and wolves. After visiting Fred, I was really excited to do a full package, which would allow me a chance at all of them.

The problem here was the price tag—$26,000. When I looked in my hunting fund, I had $0. This was not unusual for me. Part of the reason for this book is to portray the fact that the dream I eventually made a reality was done on what is sometimes quoted as "on a shoestring." I don't know exactly what that saying means, but I do know that almost every time I booked a hunt, I had exactly the same amount in my hunting account—zero.

The idea of a trip to Alaska was a huge deal for me. Previously, I had spent a few hundred dollars for an over-the-counter license in Colorado or a local deer tag in South Dakota. After a few days of thinking and a date night with Becky, she decided I could go. I would do a combo hunt of Dall sheep and barren-ground caribou in late August to early September 1992. As I am a farmer by trade, this schedule suited me as the dates fell between wheat and soybean harvest.

The total was about $8,000, all inclusive. (Most hunts after the early '90s usually included some other charges like charter flights, licenses, trophy prep, etc., that were in addition to the hunt price.) With the trip decided on and planned, there was a huge problem. Fred needed half of the money now to reserve the spot. Thus began the scenario that went on for the next sixteen years. I wrote Fred a check for $4,000. I then called the bank and said I had a big check coming through and hoped they would cover it. I always had a good relationship with my lenders. When I was overdrawn at the bank as I tried to replenish the hunting fund, I was always truthful. They trusted me because I never lied. If I said I could have the overdraft covered in two days, it was covered. There were times when I felt as though my overdraft charges were literally paying the salaries at the bank. As I reflect back to those days, I'm sure my lenders were the ones thinking "You've got to be kidding. After I returned home from this trip to Alaska, I knew two things: One, I had sheep hunting fever, and I wanted to hunt all four species of sheep. Second, I loved the whole experience of flying into the wilderness and hunting using only my two feet to get around the area. I wasn't sure how I would finance the hunts, but I knew in my heart I was going to do a huge amount of hunting from this day forward. Pretty ambitious stuff for a farmer who had gone broke in the potato business ten years earlier.

My purpose for talking about financing here is for you to get a sense of what is possible to fulfill your dream. I tried to earn extra money on the farm to support hunting. We raised many crops that were certainly not normal for our area but had a greater profit potential than the normal corn, soybeans, and wheat. Some of the different crops we tried were popcorn, dark red kidney beans, light red kidney beans, navy beans, black turtle beans, and potatoes. You've already discovered how the potatoes worked. Unbelievably, the popcorn worked very well for quite some time. We used to sell to Orville Redenbacher and delivered a very fine product. Then it happened. The summers started getting cooler, and we couldn't get the popcorn to mature anymore. So much for Al Gore's global warming. We still raise the dark red kidneys as they have been profitable for us for over twenty-five years.

Okay, I am thrilled with the fact that I am going to go sheep hunting, and I try to read all I can about how to prepare. The first thing to do is GET IN SHAPE and, as sheep hunters say, get in "sheep shape." Again, a problem as I have been on a diet most of my adult life. I think like those of us who are just too short for our weight, we have tried most of the diets out there, and like most of us, I have met with little success. Sure, I would drop a few pounds, but then I would gain them back and more. I had a standing joke with my wife that went like this: In the early 1980s, every time Becky became pregnant, I would also gain 10 pounds. She would lose hers, but I kept mine. Then in the late 1980s and 1990s, it was every time we added 1,000 acres to our farm, I would gain another 10 pounds. All right, let's do the math. I started at 160, plus the three kids put me at 190, plus the 8,000 acres added to the farm another 80, therefore, 270 pounds. Let me tell you that is not sheep shape. Oh wait, it may very well be sheep shape, all right, a pregnant ewe.

I started immediately with the jogging and dieting. I really did quite well over the winter months and shed some pounds. Long story short, sometime in early summer with about three months until the hunt, even though I was running four to six miles per day, I still needed to slim down more. What I did next may have worked better than anything I had done previously. I went to one of those hypnosis weight loss meetings, was hypnotized, and lost my cravings for sweets. The day before I left for Alaska, I weighed in at 185 pounds, and I was able to run six to eight miles. I was awfully proud of what I had done.

Sometime in June 1992, I had received the hunt package from the outfitter, Don Trautman. It included answers to the questions I had concerning the logistics of the ten days I would spend with him. There was also a list of clothing to bring and a real shocking statement: "You are only allowed to bring 60 pounds of gear with you, including your rifle." All I could think was YOU'VE GOT TO BE KIDDING. My .300 Weatherby Mark V Lazermark weighs almost 11 pounds alone, thus leaving me only 49 pounds for the rest of my gear, that is, hunting shoes, hip boots, parka, wool pants, underwear, socks, cap, gloves, shells, binoculars, a set of clean clothes for the return home, plus the bag to carry all this, which also weighed in at 4 pounds. Becky enjoyed watching and laughed as I packed and unpacked twenty or more times. I just couldn't keep it at 60 pounds. Finally, the day I left, my bag weighed in at about 70 pounds, and I ended up wearing multiple layers of clothing on my person, including a pretty heavy jacket.

You wouldn't believe the looks I got from people at the Aberdeen, South Dakota, airport as I waited to fly to Minneapolis, where I would connect to Anchorage. I am sure there were some hushed words, such as "Look at this idiot," as it was 100+ degrees outside on that August day. Yes, my bag was overweight, but I truly hoped there would be a little tolerance factor when I arrived in Deadhorse to meet Don Trautman.

I will never forget the flight into Anchorage. I had a window seat, and as we approached from the east side of the city, the view of the Chugach Mountains with all their glaciers and tall rugged peaks was just unbelievable. Next, before we landed, we flew over the Knik Arm of the Cook Inlet, which is part of the Gulf of Alaska. It just really looked like there was water everywhere. After overnighting in Anchorage, I made the three-and-a-half-hour flight to Deadhorse and Purdue Bay, which are located on the north coast of Alaska, right on the Arctic Ocean. This flight takes you over the Alaskan Range, where the mountains are even taller and more remote than the Chugach Mountains.

I also got a great view of Mt. Denali, which is North America's tallest mountain at almost twenty thousand feet. Usually obscured by clouds, I was lucky to have a sunny, cloudless day to observe the entire wilderness. Purdue Bay is a long way north, and we had left the trees (called the tree line as trees cannot grow any farther north) behind as we passed over Fairbanks and then over yet another mountain range, the Brooks Range. These mountains are unique in that there are no trees other than very short willows, and they tend to be a little less rugged than their neighbors to the south.

After landing at the Deadhorse airport, one of Don's pilots picked me up, and we drove to a smaller terminal from where he flew us to the base camp. The airplane of choice for the trip was a Cessna 206. I was thinking this would be a great experience as I had heard and read so much about the Alaskan bush pilot. What could be better than a nice, relaxing, scenic ride out to the base camp? Boy, was I wrong. The first thing I saw was the pilot adding about seven quarts of oil to the airplane motor. I know a little about small planes as I had completed, at that time, about sixty hours of flying solo in a Cessna 172. The thing that scared me was when he said he wasn't changing the oil but just adding. I just said, "YOU'VE GOT TO BE KIDDING." Wow, the motor only held a few more quarts than he was adding. I know I should have been positive, but thoughts went through my head, like this would be my first and only trip to Alaska as this plane would crash after it run out of oil. I said the first of many prayers that were part of this trip and other trips over the years.

Next, the pilot said he would be back shortly as he had to go back to the big terminal to get some more hunters. He came back with three more people, and after introductions, I learned they were from overseas. As I watched them unload their gear, my jaw dropped as I saw each person had three or four bags of luggage, which I estimated their total weight to be in excess of 200 pounds for each hunter. Did they not get the memo I got about only 60 pounds of gear?

We were instructed to bring our bags inside the small terminal so we could weigh them. I was thinking this was where I would be asked to leave something behind so I could make weight. I was thinking these foolish guys would have to leave two-thirds of what they brought. No, it wasn't to be that way at all. I weighed in at 68 pounds. The three of them had a combined total of 585 pounds, making my earlier estimate pretty close. Then the pilot said, "OK, let's start loading." What? I questioned him about the excess weight. He said, "Oh, that's okay as most hunters usually bring too much." You guessed it. I said, "YOU'VE GOT TO BE KIDDING."

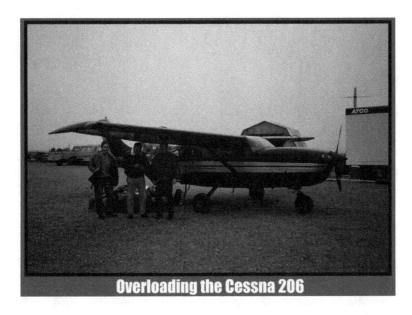

Overloading the Cessna 206

Now I can laugh about it, but at the time, the Irish heritage, which is a pretty big part of me, was boiling mad, but I didn't let it show. I was really concerned because we were going to load five guys and all this gear into the 206. We took off, knowing we were overloaded. I was too mad to be scared. We did clear the runway with just a few feet to spare. Thank God!

After about an hour, we circle over the base camp to check the wind sock before landing. I don't see a runway, so I think it's on the pilot's side of the plane. We drop, and all I see is the riverbed. Sure enough, we land on a gravel bar with water on both sides. I say to everyone, "Welcome to Alaska hunting!"

Base camp an hour flight south of Deadhorse

Don and his wife, Stasha, are very gracious hosts. After a wonderful lunch of Alaskan moose roast, we check my rifle with a few shots at one hundred yards. Next, it is time to get acquainted while I fill out the hunting licenses. Don's plan is to get me to the sheep camp today so I can hunt tomorrow. I inform him that if I indeed finish my hunt for sheep and caribou early, I had arranged to do an Alaskan moose hunt with another outfitter closer to Anchorage. I had lined this up sometime in May. I hadn't used Fred to book this hunt, and I had found the outfitter's name in some magazine ad. I had no idea what it would be like as he was a new outfitter trying to get started, and he was going to take a few hunters, but he didn't have one reference to share with me. I bought this hunt as it was relatively inexpensive, and I am a sucker for the underdog. I could see the hurt in Don's eyes as I told him this, and he asked why I hadn't added the moose with him. I tried feebly to explain the zero hunting funds, but I couldn't soothe his hurt feelings.

Don's super cub, getting ready to go to sheep camp

He then flies me to the spike camp where I will hunt Dall sheep. This time we take a Super Cub and again land on a gravel bar. The landing is rougher, but with the huge tundra tires, the plane handles the terrain easily. I meet my young guide, John, who is originally from Wyoming, and it soon feels as though we've been old friends. It is about 6:30 p.m., and he informs me it gets dark at about 11:30 p.m. Daylight is at 3:30 a.m. We glass some of the close mountains, which don't look very steep, but I know they are, and we see quite a few sheep, including some smaller rams. John says he has seen some bigger rams off farther south, and we would go there tomorrow. In Alaska, as with many Canadian provinces, you are not allowed to hunt the same day you fly. This is a good law as it keeps people from spotting animals from the air and then landing and going after them.

About 9:30 p.m., I decide I had better get some sleep as we intend to be up at 2:30 a.m. Well, of course, I am so excited to be here hunting sheep that try as I might, including counting sheep (pun intended again), I can't sleep all night. Possibly, John's snoring is a factor in my sleepless night, or maybe it's the fact that this tent is even smaller than the polar bear camp. Thoughts play over and over in my mind. Will I be able to keep up with John as we scale these mountains? Will my shooting be good if we see something of trophy size? Did I bring the right clothes? Will I be able to keep warm? It goes on and on.

Sheep mountains in the Brooks Range

As for keeping up with the guide, I learned on this hunt, and it was true for all the hunts that followed, that even though I may have trained very hard, it is almost impossible to be in as good a shape as the guides. They simply work the mountains every day, which makes them extremely fit.

At 3:30 a.m., we start our hike up the mountain. Yes, they are much steeper than they look, and they are very dangerous today because we have light rain, which makes the rocks we are stepping on and over very slick. At about 11:30 a.m., we approach somewhat of a summit. I am feeling pretty good considering the eight-hour climb to this point.

Almost as if John had planned it, there is a band of Dall rams bedded not more than seventy-five yards below us. "YOU'VE GOT TO BE KIDDING." I can't believe they didn't hear my heavy breathing as we approached the top. The biggest ram is very nice with broomed horns, and I quickly learn the importance of being ready to shoot at any time while big game hunting. The rams all stand as I am sure they have caught a whiff of my perspiration-soaked clothes, and with one quick shot, I have my ram.

The beginning of "sheep fever"

Before leaving home, I had made the decision that if I were fortunate enough to take a ram, I would have the guide remove the entire hide so I could do a life-size mount. My reasoning was that this would be the only sheep hunt I would ever do. I had figured to hunt the remaining three sheep species required substantially more than $0 in a hunt fund. As my hunting career unfolded, the full-size hide was a very good decision as I eventually life-size mounted fourteen species of my North American 29.

We took pictures, loaded, and started down the mountain with full packs, carrying all the meat, the horns, and the full hide. I was certainly glad I had gotten in pretty good shape as going down was almost as hard as the climb. The good news was it had stopped raining, so the slippery rocks were not an issue. A fog had rolled in, and I was glad we had my ram as we couldn't see the top anymore.

We got back about 7:30 p.m., and Don showed up at the camp with the Super Cub. I guess he must have sensed we would be lucky, so I loaded my gear and my ram, and we headed back to the base camp. I only got to spend one night in the sheep camp but was okay with that.

As we took off, Don said over the radio, "As long as we get through the pass, we will be okay." At this point, I was thinking, *And if we don't make it through the pass, then what?* The fog was practically on the ground now, and Don's words to me shook me to the core. He said, "Can you watch out your side of the plane for the mountain?" I said, "YOU'VE GOT TO BE KIDDING!" Okay, I watched, but I hoped I wouldn't see the mountain as a crash would be imminent. We did make it through, and there was no fog on the other side, so the trip back to the base camp provided a wondrous look at some of the finest the Brooks Range has to offer. Reflecting on the day's events, I now had what is known in hunting circles as sheep fever. From that moment on, wild sheep would forever be my favorite.

When I arrived for breakfast, after a great sleep, the three overseas hunters, a hunter from the East Coast, and Don and Stasha were inside the lodge. After the customary congratulations from the group on my ram, we all swapped stories about our hunting careers. I had the shortest list of accomplishments with the exception of our East Coast friend. It seemed this was his very first big game hunt. He had booked the total combo hunt, the one I wanted to do, and he had gone out yesterday to try for caribou. He and his guide had spent the day hiking around camp, but they had returned early. Evidently, he was not at all thrilled with the idea of walking and climbing just to get a wild animal. With that said, he had informed Don that he was quitting and wanted to leave. To me, this was unbelievable as he had spent $26,000 plus the cost of his flight from New York to Anchorage and hunted part of one day. At this point, this was the number 1 "YOU'VE GOT TO BE KIDDING" moment for this trip.

After this incident, the overseas guys figured it was time for their complaints. They let Stasha know that they expected clean sheets on their beds every night. They also would not be getting up early as they had come to party. Now I didn't realize we were staying at the

Hilton, and I wondered what they were going to do when they got to the spike camp and slept on the ground in their little tent with the guide only inches away. You think I sound a little bitter over the excess baggage, don't you? Well, sort of, but I actually had gotten over that as I realized I had enough gear in my 68#'s to keep from freezing to death. I was still a little hurt when I saw that a large part of their excess baggage was special liquor.

After lunch that day, I got a new guide who was going to take me around the mountains close to the camp to try for caribou. The caribou had been migrating through in pretty good numbers, so we had a good chance at getting one. We climbed a small hill, started to glass, and found little groups here and there. One lone bull was quite a way out, but he looked pretty good. My guide tried to educate me about caribou, in that there are three things that make them trophy size. First is their top points, second their bezzes, and third the mass and the spread. He said it was hard to get all three to be good, but usually, you get two out of three.

The other important aspect of the actual hunt was not to try to chase them down from behind but rather to cut them off. We found another great bull, and he was moving. I decided to go for him. After about thirty minutes, as we were getting closer, he did something caribou don't often do. He lay down and went to sleep, right there in front of us. My guide told me to go alone from this point. It looked like this would be easier than I thought, so I proceeded to get down among the grass and very short willows and crawled toward him. He looked good as his bezzes were huge, the mass was good, but the tops were poor, and so was the spread. I continued the stalk until I was only ten yards away and he remained asleep. I waited about thirty minutes, he stood, and with one shot, I had my caribou. The ground shrinkage was a little more than I had hoped, but incredibly, I had come to Alaska for two species, and I was done in two days. This really set the pace for the rest of my hunting career as I typically was very fortunate (okay, very lucky) and got the animals I sought with a few exceptions, which you will read about later in the book. We made the hike back to the base camp, and I spent the night. The next day, the same 206 I originally arrived in from Deadhorse returned to take me back to Purdue Bay. Yes, it was still flying, but I had no idea of the amount of oil it took this time.

It's hard to miss at only ten yards!

While at the base camp, Stasha had arranged for my airline ticket to be changed so I could return to Anchorage seven days early. I am going to meet the other outfitter in two days, so after landing in Anchorage, I rent a car and drive to Palmer, Alaska, where the state fair is going on. You have never experienced anything like this. The pictures you see on TV do not do justice to the actual size of the vegetables they are able to produce because of the twenty-four hours of daylight. The fact that I am a farmer made this especially exciting for me, and I asked the local producers many questions on fertilizer, chemicals, and irrigation.

My moose hunt began about an hour north of Anchorage. The outfitter has lined up a local pilot to fly us out to a lake near Mt. Susitna. The local pilot asks my outfitter some questions about his experience and length of time as an outfitter. He doesn't like the answers he's getting, and to sum up, he refuses to fly us all the way to Mt. Susitna. He says he is responsible for our safety and will need to check on us more often because of the lack of experience.

Now once again, I have that feeling of uncertainty I've had a few times since I got to Alaska. The worst of this situation is I have no one to blame but myself as I had bypassed the proper way to do things when I hadn't used Fred or at least made sure this outfitter had at least one good reference. The local pilot knew of a lake close by; he would fly us there and drop us off. This became my only choice, and I wasn't happy. It became hard to find anything good about this hunt. The rain never stopped, which happens on hunts, but the outfitters tent was full of holes, and our clothes and sleeping bags were wet. His hip boots leaked, so he was limited to a few miles of walking daily before the blisters would shut him down. He had brought enough food for about two days instead of being prepared for a week or even ten days. Our hunting territory consisted of one small lake in a vast area of heavy timber. I don't even know if there were any moose in the area as we never saw or heard any.

After four days, I was concerned about hypothermia because everything was wet, and we had no way to dry out. I am not a quitter, but at times, you have to be a realist. I asked if he would put the blue tarp down to signal the pilot to pick us up. This is the classic example of you get what you pay for in life. It was a hard lesson to learn, but I learned well.

In January of 1991, I attended my first Safari Club International (SCI) convention and attended every year after. I never had a bad hunting experience again, with the exception of this one and one other you will read about later. After 1992, I hunted only with outfitters who were SCI members, and I was able to personally check out the outfitter before I booked a hunt, including references. I also learned the value of the booking agent and used them on every hunt. Fred ended up venturing into new businesses, so I began to use Jeff Blair of Blair Worldwide Hunting and Gregg Severinson of Cabela's Outdoor Adventures. Both of these provided the very best services for me.

So back in Anchorage, I have a thought. (My wife says I think too much.) My idea is as long as I am here in Alaska, I would still like to take a moose. There are two problems: one, I don't have an outfitter, and two, the hunting fund is still at zero. I decide to call Don Trautman and explain what happened. He laughs, not at me but at the situation. I ask if there is any way possible he could fit me in at such short notice to do a moose hunt. He says if I can get there the next day, the season opens in the Brooks Range, and the spot left by the East Coast hunter is open. It was great news for me as I only have to pay half price for the hunt, and Don will take my check, which I will cover when I get home. That leaves the last problem. I need six hundred and some odd dollars for another round-trip ticket from Anchorage to Purdue Bay. I make the call to Pat at the bank in South Dakota and explain my dilemma, and he agrees to put the money in my checking account so I can pay for the ticket.

I really had a pretty good relationship with the banks I worked with, even though earlier in this chapter, it may not have sounded that way. My success in dealing with banks was because I never told them lies. If I was overdrawn, and I was too often (my overdraft charges actually paid the bank employees' salary), when I said I had money coming in to cover the overdraft, I always made sure it happened when I said it would.

So now I have everything in place, and in the morning, I return to Purdue Bay. This time Don picks me up at the airport, and we take the same 206 to camp. It is still flying, and I ask Don about the motor. He says it uses a little oil. What can I say? After the same routine as last time, we head out to the moose camp located east of the base camp along the Canning River. The flight is spectacular as the sun is shining, and bull moose can be seen from miles away as they have just removed the velvet from their horns. With the sun reflecting off those six- to seven-foot-wide horns, they look like satellite dishes. Don says at times, they can be seen from ten miles. What a sight! We land again on a gravel bar, and I meet Ray, who will be my guide. He is camped here as there is a very good bull in the area. After an early dinner, we hike a few miles down the river and spot him with a herd of cows. It is September 4, and the rut is going full force. Since I have flown today, we will have to wait until morning and try to locate him again.

Three foot tall wiilows are giants in the Brooks Range

We rise about three thirty and set out to locate the big bull. The morning is beautiful with a little frost but sun and no wind. At six thirty, we find him still holding his harem together. The sight of those huge antlers shining in the morning sun is a memory I will never forget. After a short stalk and some grunting to imitate another moose, I am able to take the shot, and I have my Alaskan moose. He is a dandy with horns at sixty-four inches wide. I am thrilled, but Ray asks if I am OK. I say yes, but I can't keep the tears away. I am just thinking how blessed I have been my entire life and how God rewards perseverance. My months of planning, running, dieting, and praying have all been worth it as Don has made this an experience of a lifetime.

Now the reality sets in. We look at this huge animal, and I wonder how in the world we handle such a creature. Ray estimate he weighs 1,600 pounds, and we have to move him somewhat to get pictures. After pictures, we spend all day and most of the evening to debone meat, remove the hide and horns, and get it hauled back to our tent site.

Ray and I made seven trips back and forth to get it all done, crossing streams about twelve times each trip. We were exhausted by the time we finished. On or about the third trip with full backpacks, we had company. Three grizzly bears—yes, three, not one—flanked us about 150 yards away. They could obviously smell the fresh moose meat and wanted a part of it. They followed us back and forth for a few trips and then quietly went away. I didn't have a tag for grizzly and could not afford the trophy fee to Don even if I had taken one.

At 64" nearly as tall as the hunter

As an old hunting saying goes, "The things you see when you don't have a tag." Ray and I finished hauling at 12:30 a.m., and we were exhausted.

We awoke about six o'clock to a rainy, foggy, and windy morning. I was outside and realized I was wearing all the warm clothes on my person that I had brought with me, and I was shivering and couldn't stop. I don't know why, but I was suddenly very scared and prayed that I would survive, even though I was in no immediate danger. I made a mental note that day to purchase the very best clothing I could afford as until that moment, I had never been too particular about brands, etc. There is a huge difference in clothing, and as you will learn in later chapters, the Alaska weather is typically much different from what I had experienced on this hunt.

Rule # 1 when you take pictures: Don't sit on your trophy

The weather turned sunny, and Don arrived about nine o'clock with the Super Cub. Once again, I was not sure how he knew I had my moose, but here he was again just like after the sheep hunt, and I was so glad to see him. We loaded my gear and some of the moose meat and headed back to camp. He returned later to bring the rest of the meat, the horns, and the hide. We enjoyed moose steaks for dinner that evening, and they were much better than any elk I've had. The next morning, we headed to Purdue Bay again with the Super Cub. We had a full load as I took the Dall ram, the caribou, and the moose with me. The horns of the moose were too big to go inside, so Don strapped them to a strut on the outside of the plane. Now this led into another "YOU'VE GOT TO BE KIDDING" moment. As we approached the Deadhorse airport, I heard the tower tell Don to use runway 31, but as we came down, I saw Don was using runway 13. I asked, "Is this the wrong way?" He said, "I have to land this way so the tower can't see the moose horns on the outside of the plane. You don't want them to confiscate your horns, do you?" Thus ends my first trip to Alaska. I don't know how it could have been any better.

The final "YOU'VE GOT TO BE KIDDING" moment happened in the Minneapolis airport terminal after I got in from

Anchorage. I was changing planes, and it was a real small plane that took us to South Dakota, so you had to claim your luggage. Now I had all my gear on one of those pushcarts, including the horns of all three animals, with the moose horns right on top of a pretty big pile. A very nice woman walked up to me, pointed at the moose horns, and asked, "Did you get that white-tailed deer up north by Hibbing, Minnesota?" Well, what could I say? I just agreed with her and said, "They have some really big ones up there, don't they?"

CHAPTER 3

Speed Goats

As I have mentioned, I grew up in a loving Catholic family with wonderful siblings. Two of my brothers, Steve and Dave, are also big game hunters. I have enjoyed their company on many hunts. Dave was part of this hunt in Gillette, Wyoming. It is the first week in October 1992, and we are here to hunt antelope (alias speed goats) and also Rocky Mountain mule deer. I spent a few weeks on the farm after returning from the Alaska hunt. I had time to harvest most of the soybeans before I left, and my wonderful wife, Becky, and our hired help were going to finish them up. The soybean crop was very poor this year as we had had a very unusual late frost in May, and we had had to replant the entire farm in early June. The summer was cooler than usual, which, when coupled with an early freeze in September, led to a pretty small yield. My banker was hoping we would get enough crop income to reduce our outstanding debt, but it was not going to happen this year. Our favorite saying in the farm industry at times like these is "There's always next year." When I get back from this hunt, we will start corn harvest, and hopefully, the corn will yield better than the beans.

The past January 1991, Becky and I attended the SCI convention for our first time. I knew then I was going to Alaska in August 1992, but we were talking about some hunt we could do together. My wife has never been a good flier, so we thought about a hunt closer to home that we could just drive to. We met Marion and Mary Scott at the SCI convention. They ran a very successful outfitting business north of Gillette, Wyoming, which for us is about a seven-hour drive.

Along with being one of the very best places to meet fantastic outfitters, SCI also conducts daily auctions at their conventions. Outfitters will donate hunts to SCI, and then they are auctioned to the highest bidder in a live forum. The outfitters typically get enough back to cover their costs, and the rest goes to SCI to help promote animal habitat. The system works very well for both parties and usually allows a hunter to get a bit of a reduced price for a hunt. Anyway, the Scotts had a combination hunt for antelope and mule deer for two hunters on the auction. Becky and I were the successful bidders.

We had talked to the Scotts before the auction, and they seemed like our kind of people as they were also farmers and ranchers. A sidenote here: a few years later, Marion and Mary were awarded one of the highest honors to be given by SCI when they were named the Professional Hunters of North America. This honor is given to only one outfitter each year, and there are thousands in North America. So you can see how prestigious this was for them. Becky and I were thrilled to have our hunt lined up with the Scotts and looking forward to doing it together.

On the return trip back to South Dakota from the convention, Becky kind of turned cold to the idea of shooting her own animals and didn't want to be gone from home at that time of the year because of all the kids' school projects. So she decided that someone else should go in her place. I fully understood her reasoning but still wanted her to experience a guided hunt. She was able, a few years later, to join me on numerous hunts as a spectator. Therefore, the search was on to find someone who wanted to go to Wyoming, and my brother Dave was glad to accept the offer.

My brother and I have hunted together quite a few times. We've done elk and deer in Montana as well as elk in Oregon, Colorado, and New Mexico. I would call both of us trophy hunters as we have come home without animals many, many times, even though there were plenty that could have been taken. On one occasion in Colorado when hunting in the Flat Tops Wilderness, we had made an eight-hour climb up Mitchell Creek and spotted a huge bull elk. We tried very hard to get to it but seemed like the higher we climbed, the farther away we were, but we weren't giving up. Along the way, we stumbled upon a huge mule deer that we could have taken, but our sights were set on the elk. Well, a mere three hours later, we realized we weren't going to get a chance at the elk, so we didn't get the deer or the elk.

I would venture to say that hunters in general may be the most optimistic people on the planet. You never hear conversations that start like "Well, I know I'll never get anything big." They usually begin with "I'm not going to take anything little," meaning, of course, that most of us are truly trophy hunters. I mean no disrespect to the true meat hunter, and I thank God for them as animal populations require thinning at times. In all actuality, without the meat hunter, there would be increased competition for food supplies, thus a reduced number of trophy-size animals. So thank you, meat hunters.

Here in Wyoming, we are hunting "speed goats" and mule deer. A typical day includes starting early in the morning to locate deer and then toward midday to concentrate on "speed goats." Our guide, Doug, is a local and knows the country very well. He is a cowboy, and using his ability, he is able to show us hundreds of animals. Once again, Dave and I are trophy hunting, and Doug knows it. He has been such a good sport, although I think there are a few times he thought we should have taken a shot. We really just wanted to take home good animals. The days would evolve around searching and spotting mule deer and antelope until dark. The Scotts would then provide an open bar and wonderful food.

After day 3, which was the halfway point of the hunt, I was getting a little frustrated, but I shouldn't have been. Like I mentioned, we had literally seen hundreds of deer and antelope. How could it be any better? I was pretty naive in thinking that by purchasing the auction hunt at SCI, there would be trophy animals over every hill. That is not how it works. Trophies are only a small percentage of any given population, and you have to have perseverance to find them. A little luck is also very welcome. I was just a little spoiled by the Alaska trip in that I got all trophies that scored high enough to be entered in SCI's record books.

Now we were discussing with Doug the possibility of going into Gillette to the local bar and having what my brother Dave likes to call attitude adjustment. Well, we went to "the cowboy bar," got home very late, and talked about hunting until about 4:00 a.m. We were back out hunting at 6:00 a.m.

The attitude adjustment worked great as by 8:30 a.m., Dave had his speed goat. He made a fantastic long-running shot. The goat was a real beauty and scored high enough to make the Boone and Crockett record book. I had decided to let Dave, his nickname is Herb, have the first shot as I had been so lucky in Alaska, and he had not had too much luck hunting of late. After Herb's shot, Doug went to go to work, prepping the goat. He was not fully over attitude-adjustment night, and we felt sorry for him as the smell of the goat sent him to the side of the truck to talk to the outside lavatory. He was mumbling something about being poisoned. *Yeah right,* we thought, *maybe alcohol poisoning.* The sight of him really made us all pretty queasy.

Herb and his attitude adjustment antelope

Less than an hour later, we spotted another great antelope buck in a different herd, and I had my goat. He was almost as big as Herb's, and I was thrilled. My shooting was poor, but I did take him on the third shot. They just seem like they are always on the move, and I hadn't shot at many moving targets. By this time, Doug was feeling much better and got his work done without interruption.

The following day, I took a very nice mule deer at first light,

and Herb took his that afternoon. His was just a bit smaller, so the brotherly competition on this hunt ended a tie. All the other hunters in the camp were also very successful, and one of the last things Marion and Mary asked us to do before we left the camp was to fill out an SCI hunt report. Once again, I was naive about trophy quantities, and I filled it out by giving the Scotts low marks for trophy availability. I hadn't spent enough time thinking about it before I put my thoughts down.

Doug and I with my "speed goat"

I don't know what I was thinking, but Mary was very quick to look over the report and said to me, "YOU'VE GOT TO BE KIDDING." She asked if I would reconsider as the reports are so critical for their business to succeed. "Absolutely," I told her. They had provided us an opportunity to take two antelope that were certainly way above average and two mule deer that were at least better than average. In the end, I felt terrible for not giving them great marks the first time. They had run such a good camp and provided us with a great guide. We left as good friends, and Becky and I would visit with them at subsequent SCI conventions.

This is a good time to talk about guides. As mentioned in chapter 1, I have been on forty-plus guided hunts. I have always enjoyed and have great respect for anyone who guides big game hunters. They have to be psychologists, babysitters, hard workers, and good listeners. I have never questioned my guide's decisions, even though at times, I wasn't sure if I was physically able to go where we needed to go, for example, on sheep hunting when he might say we needed to go back down the same mountain we had just scaled for ten hours and go up the next one as the sheep had crossed over. Guides have a very hard job keeping the hunter's morale going when animals cannot be seen or, as in the case here in Wyoming, there are lots of animals but just a few trophies.

Rocky Mountain "Mulie"

I have always had pretty good luck while hunting, and I attribute that to working with the guide and being as pleasant as possible. It just makes things go better. Doug was an excellent guide, and coupled with a few prayers, we ended very successfully. The final day of the hunt, we had time to do something I had never done. Doug took us out to shoot wild turkey. Great fun! I now see the excitement many hunters get as turkey season approaches every year.

A few years later, Doug made a visit to the farm in South Dakota. It was mid-November, and we were in the middle of the local deer season. We saw lots of deer, but there were no trophy-size bucks. It would seem trophy hunting is basically the same, no matter the location. After the Wyoming trip, I had two more species of North American animals, bringing my total to six species. I couldn't wait to go hunting again but had nothing lined up as the hunting fund was very low, empty actually.

Herb's nice mule deer

CHAPTER 4

Stoney

During the winter of 1992 and into early 1993, I spent a great deal of time thinking of ways to finance another sheep hunt. I wanted to hunt another species of wild sheep. It appeared to me that the only way it was going to happen was either to win the lottery (I actually have zero chance of winning the lottery as I don't buy tickets) or come up with some creative financing.

I'm not sure which friend told me about cancellation hunts, but I started to check them out. Cabela's had a program you could sign up for. You might get a reduced price if you could pack your bags and go hunting on very, very short notice. When I say short, I mean they call you today, and you are on your way tomorrow. Most of the booking agents also offered some price reductions when one of their clients couldn't make a hunt. Usually, the agent had time to find someone, thereby giving most of the money back to the original hunter. I went ahead and signed up at Cabela's and with Jeff Blair. I really wasn't expecting anything to happen, but the free price for this service fit my hunting fund, which, as I'll bet you guessed, was empty.

We had a very busy spring on the farm, and things started out very good. The weather was almost ideal, and we got the crop planted in good time. We prayed that Mother Nature wouldn't deal us the blow we got last year, with the late frost in May and the early frost in September. We really needed a good crop this year to make up for the losses last year.

Sometime in June, I got a call from Cabela's Outdoor Adventures. They asked if was interested in doing a hunt in British Columbia for Stone sheep. I said, "Am I interested? YOU'VE GOT TO BE

KIDDING." The price was reduced by only a few thousand dollars, but that was good enough to get me excited. The dates were July 29 to August 12.

I had so many things to do to get ready. My brothers Steve and Dave (nicknamed Herb, and I don't know why) and I have been involved in the custom harvest industry since 1974. This business is where you go on the road with your harvest equipment and harvest other farmers' crops for a fee. Our operation has grown to be one of the largest in the United States. We were harvesting about one hundred thousand acres per year, stretching from North Texas to Canada, along with doing our own crops in South Dakota and North Dakota. We were operating up to ten new John Deere combines and all the support equipment. This included three tractors, three grain carts, and fifteen semitrucks.

Our new combines

Anyway, we had taken on a new custom harvest job in South Dakota of about ten thousand acres. This job was to start around July 15 and continue until about August 5 if the weather cooperated. I could see a conflict in dates with the proposed sheep hunt, but I just had to figure a plan that would allow me to go sheep hunting. As it turned out, we got quite a bit of rain during the end of July, so we had over five thousand acres left to do on July 29 when I was expected to leave for the hunt. I called the outfitter and asked if I could show up a few days late, and he said fine. I would not be able to add the days to the end but would shorten up my hunt by the days I was late. Oh well, what could I do?

After all the trouble to negotiate a late arrival, it seemed everything would work out great. Boy, was I wrong. That night, we ended up getting eight inches of rain on our South Dakota farm, and we had a flood. We didn't get it out in Central South Dakota where we were harvesting. Thank God! We had to pump basements at our houses, get irrigation systems unstuck, help people move cattle, and get equipment moved around from standing water. It was an unbelievable mess. It looked as if I would have to miss the hunt altogether.

But after all this, my two brothers said they would cover for me and told me to go hunt. They were always very supportive of my goals, and I loved them dearly for this. We had nothing mature enough to harvest on our farm, and there was no need to irrigate because of all the rain. That would leave Becky able to cover for me on the farm.

Darwin's beautiful float plane

On August 2, I left for Watson Lake, Yukon, Canada. The trip was from Aberdeen to Minneapolis; and then to Vancouver, British Columbia; and then to Watson Lake. Darwin Carey, the owner of Scoop Lake Outfitters, met me at Watson Lake. We took the short one-hour flight in Darwin's floatplane to Scoop Lake, located in Northern British Columbia.

We followed the Turnagain River, and I quickly saw why it was so named. We landed safely at the base camp, and I met Wendy, Darwin's wife, and enjoyed a unique meal of wild sheep ribs. I had never had it before, and it was wonderful. After sighting the rifle and repacking, we loaded the floatplane for the flight out to Colt Lake.

There, I met my guide and his wrangler, both of whom would help me for the next ten days. The wrangler would take care of the horses each morning and evening. He had quite a job as when we got in for the day, he would put hobbles on the horses' front feet and bells around their neck and turn them out for the night. At about three thirty, he was up and trying to track them down. Sometimes they would be a few miles away. I was glad to have him doing that instead of myself or the guide.

We hunted around Colt Lake for three days. We would ride the horses into different valleys and glass for rams. When we would find something promising, we would throw the backpacks on and climb the mountains to get a better look at the different rams. We hadn't found anything big enough (they had to be at least a full curl), so we decided to move to another camp. This took most of day 4. We then hunted two days in the new place and saw many sheep but, again, no rams. We spent most of time climbing and getting to the tops so we could view the countryside by looking down instead of up. Up until this point, my guide had not been impressed with my glassing ability. I just literally couldn't find the sheep in my binoculars. They had a bit of a blue-black hue to their color, and many of the mountainsides were also of the same hue. Anyway, on this day, I actually found quite a few rams myself and finally gained his respect. He actually chuckled all the times he would try to point out where he was looking at sheep, and I couldn't pick them up. He also chuckled one day as we were climbing a very large peak, and it was quite warm. I had stripped down to my skivvies as I tried to keep up with my young guide. He told me he had never had a hunter strip down to just his underwear.

Colt Lake from above, a six hour climb

Hey, you do what you have to do not to be embarrassed by your lack of climbing ability. I was in poor shape for this hunt as I had gained 35 pounds since I had returned from Alaska and the Dall sheep hunt. I really missed weighing 185 like I did for that hunt. I vowed I would never go sheep hunting again without making some kind of reasonable effort to be in shape. I had been spoiled in Alaska with my one-day hunt. This was not to be here in British Columbia. I really was exhausted every night. We spent day 7 in the tent because of rain and foggy conditions. I knew that I was not a very patient man, and this proved the point. I had a terrible time staying occupied the entire day and night. The next morning turned sunny, and we tried some new country but once again had no luck. We decided to head back to Colt Lake where we had started on day 1. On this trip, I gained a new respect for the horses. I have ridden horses on other hunts in the United States, but these horses could go places that just amazed me, including some very narrow trails along sheer cliffs. Much of the distance we covered at night, and we arrived at the cabin late that same night.

In British Columbia, any resident is allowed hunting access to most of the province. The outfitters cannot stop a resident from flying in and hunting their areas. While we were away from Colt Lake for the four days, two residents from Southeast British Columbia had flown in on their floatplane, landed on Colt Lake, and used Darwin's camp to hunt sheep. This setup isn't appreciated by the outfitters, but what do you do? The two hunters were kind enough to take a knife and scratch on the wall of the cabin that they had taken a short climb outside the camp and taken two forty-inch Stone sheep. I just shook my head and said to the guide, "YOU'VE GOT TO BE KIDDING." We had been climbing and hunting for eight days, and how ironic, the sheep were right here.

Beautiful British Columbia

Therefore, with two days left of the hunt, the guide decided we should try a spot in the opposite direction from where the locals had taken their rams. We worked very hard and saw lots of sheep, including many rams, but none were legal to take. As day 10 ended,

I was feeling a little depressed as the next day, we would leave for the base camp, and my hunt was over. This is why most sheep hunts are fourteen days long. I had cut mine to ten days because of excess rain on the farm. In these ten days, we really had seen many, many sheep with lots of rams. I was glad to have had the experience. My guide and the wrangler had done their very best and kept me cheered up for the entire time.

Stone sheep habitat

When Darwin showed with the floatplane the next morning to pick me up, he asked how it went. Well, I'm not one to hold back my words, and I usually talk before I think, so I really started in on Darwin about the locals coming and taking the two huge rams. Now I already knew he couldn't defend himself on the point, so I don't know why I brought it up the way I did. The better way to have handled it would have been to thank him for having good people, great equipment, and horses and providing an opportunity to be in the wilderness and never feeling unsafe. After saying the things I said, it surprised me that he was still willing to fly me back to the base camp.

We started across Colt Lake with the plane, and he was zigzagging back and forth across the lake. This went on for fifteen minutes, and finally, I asked what he was doing.

Doing Zig-Zags on Colt Lake

He said because there was no wind and the water was like glass he had to create manmade waves. It is nearly impossible for floatplanes to take off from the water with glass-like conditions because the floats can't break the surface tension of the water. I didn't know this and so learned something interesting.

We arrived at the base camp in time for another one of Wendy's great meals. I had a hot shower and was enjoying the company of a few hunters who had just arrived. They were going out to camp later that day. I talked in the last chapter about all hunters being optimistic, and they were all talking about how they were going to take trophy animals. I agreed with them that they were out there. About 2:00 p.m., it looked like Darwin had forgiven me and my big mouth and started visiting with me. He said he had an extra guide as a sheep hunter had taken his ram in only a few days. He wondered if I could stay a few more days and hunt right from the base camp. Could I? "Absolutely," I told him. Therefore, it was decided that in the morning, the new guide and I would take a long horse ride to Moody Lake.

We started out about 4:00 a.m., and I wondered how the horses got by so well in the dark. I guess it's just another one of God's miracles. This ride turned out to be quite long as we didn't get to any kind of sheep country until almost 2:00 p.m. We then made a climb straight up a very steep mountain. The horses were working very hard, but my guide said we had to push to get where we needed to be. He knew the area well as he usually had a tent camp here. I

45

really was a little concerned about the horses slipping and taking a spill with me on top.

High above Colt Lake

We got to a summit and got off and started to glass. The usual blue-black color was everywhere, and we were seeing sheep. We looked for about one hour when suddenly, my guide said, "I have found your ram. He is standing in that patch of cottonwoods." I thought he was kidding as I had never seen even one of these sheep anywhere close to trees, but sure enough, there he was. After some discussion about the fact he was big enough and after a short stalk, I took my ram with one shot from my Weatherby. I was thrilled, and he was a beautiful dark color. Not quite as dark as some, but how could I think of complaining? I knew he was a good sheep and didn't worry about measuring right then. It was 5:30 p.m., and we had to get pictures plus get the entire hide for a life-size mount. As mentioned in chapter 2, I was going to life-size all my sheep, no matter if I got only one or all four of them.

We could not ride the horses down the mountain as it was too steep, so it took us a long time to walk down. It was after dark when we started toward the base camp, and I knew we were in for a long night. Did I care? No, I just thanked God for my success and knew my horse would be just fine in the dark. I actually dosed off a few times while in the saddle. By the time we got back, it was already midmorning. It was a Saturday, and Darwin said we couldn't get the sheep horn inspected and plugged at Game and Fish until Monday, so it would be two days in the base camp. I didn't care as I was so glad that Darwin had been kind enough to let me stay on longer. He took the time to measure my ram, and he scored 163 and change, even though one side was broomed. He then gave me the bad news that the horn length on the one side measured 40.5 inches. I asked why that was bad. "Well," he said, "if you looked at your contract, for any sheep taken over 40 inches, there is a trophy fee." I looked at him, smiled, and said, "YOU'VE GOT TO BE KIDDING." Well, I tried to argue that the one side being broomed took the measurement down to less than 40 inches. That didn't fly, but I was actually happy that I owed the $1,000 as I had really had taken a great ram.

40.5" Stone Sheep

On Monday, the trip to the conservation office went great with the guys congratulating me on a great ram. The rest of the return trip was uneventful except when I tried to bring the sheep horns onto the airplane as a carry-on bag. I was allowed to do it, but it took a bit of negotiating. They didn't fit in the overhead, so they let me keep them kind of under the seat in front of me. I just didn't want to take the chance they would end up as lost baggage. I don't know why I was so insistent on this point as we all know airlines never lose your luggage.

Becky welcomes me home in Aberdeen, South Dakota

CHAPTER 5

Crash And Burn

I thought my luck was very good a year ago when I was able to take advantage of the cancellation spot for my Stone sheep hunt to British Columbia. Imagine how excited I was when Jeff Blair of Blair Worldwide Hunting called in October of 1994 and said they had had a cancellation, and there was a spot open to hunt Rocky Mountain bighorn sheep in Alberta, Canada. At first, I had a hard time believing that I would be lucky enough to get a chance at another sheep, but John Gates, who worked with Jeff, assured me that it was the real deal. As usual, there was a slight kink in the plan but nothing insurmountable. I had to leave immediately to keep the spot. Now for those of you reading this who own your own business, sometimes it can be hard to just take off at a moment's notice and leave the business for two weeks, especially during October, which is our harvest season on the farm.

Luckily for me, I had now gone on enough wilderness hunts that packing had become a little easier. In fact, I could get ready in about an hour as most of the items I needed were the same as the last hunt. Sometimes I needed waders, or the weather may be a little colder, so warmer clothes were needed. However, after washing clothes, the Cabela's duffel bag stayed packed from one trip to the next.

After I returned the year before from taking my Stone sheep, I had seven species of North American animals. It was interesting that I had used the same rifle on all the previous hunts, not by design, but it just happened to be that way. Therefore, this time, once again, my rifle of choice was the .300 Weatherby Mark V Lazermark. This also made packing faster as I knew I would be using the same bullets, the 180-grain Nosler Partition. This combination of rifle and bullet

49

had done such a fine job for me so far that I wasn't about to change. I really saved myself considerable money by not going and purchasing different rifles for different hunts. Given my usual financial position, the rifle-purchasing fund was as empty as the hunting fund.

As it turns out, the above combination of rifle and bullet would eventually be used to take all my 29 species. I really never planned this, but it always worked so well that I never looked at any other option. Although this scenario is certainly not the norm in the hunting world, I was very glad to have done it. I am sure that of the 120 hunters recognized for the North American 29, there are probably a very small number who have used only one rifle. I know of only one beside myself, that being J. Y. Jones, of whom I spoke in earlier chapters. His rifle of choice was the .30-06 Remington Model 700. I wasn't even aware of Mr. Jones's endeavor to collect all the North American species until I had completed mine. My three children and my son-in-law purchased his book *One Man, One Land, One Rifle* as a Christmas present in 2008.

On this hunt, I was heading to the Willmore Wilderness area of Alberta. This is located south and west of Grande Cache, Alberta. It is north of the very beautiful Jasper National Park and in and along the big Smoky River. I had to very quickly put my plan together to leave again from Aberdeen, South Dakota, and then fly to Minneapolis and then to Edmonton, Alberta. There, I had a very short five-hour stay at a motel before going downtown to catch a bus for the five-hour trip to Grande Cache, where I was to meet the outfitter, Gary Krueger. This was a fast, organized, and simple plan. I had to make arrangements to cover all the harvesting aspects going on at the farm for the next two weeks. As usual, Becky took over and assured me everything would be fine.

Oh, did I forget I also had to have a plan for paying for the hunt, which, thank God, was only half the price of the normal $13,500 or $6,500? As I look back, the price was incredibly reasonable as today, the same hunt sells for $39,000. The time right before harvest on our farm was typically the time of the year when we had the least available cash. I had called my new banker, Dan, earlier in the week and asked if he could increase my credit line by $7,500 to cover some extra expense I was expecting as I completed the harvest of our crops. I was expecting the corn to be very wet and needed the extra money for propane to dry it before storing. He had agreed and was sending it out in the next few days. Therefore, I kind of borrowed it and used the money to go hunt. As it turned out, we had very good weather, and the corn dried in the field without the use of any propane, so I had my financial miracle.

As I boarded the plane in Aberdeen, I couldn't have been any more excited. The opportunity to hunt any species of mountain sheep for me was just as good as winning the lottery. In the back of my mind, I was thinking about the grand slam of sheep. If I was successful this time, I would have three species, and this is known in sheep hunting circles as the three-quarter slam. I would only need a desert bighorn to complete my slam, but the chances of this were very slim. The odds are very, very low of drawing one of the hunting tags in any of the Western states that have huntable populations of desert bighorns. There has been some talk of Old Mexico reopening some areas for sheep, but nothing as of this date.

Watertown, South Dakota, lies about thirty minutes east of Aberdeen by air, and today the plane was scheduled to land there and pick up additional passengers. As we were making our final approach, the plane suddenly picked up speed, and we aborted the landing. There were about fifteen minutes of suspense as we circled the airport. Finally, the pilot relayed to us that the landing gear was not working, and we were going to burn up some fuel before trying to land. I couldn't help but think to myself, YOU'VE GOT TO BE KIDDING. I was starting to wonder if the airplane gods had something out for me after the crazy experiences when I hunted in Alaska.

Actually, I should really be feeling lucky as it certainly turned out much better on those Alaskan flights than I would have believed. We circled Watertown for what seemed like an hour, and the pilot relayed that we were going to try the landing. Everyone braced for the worst as we got close to the runway, and I said a prayer, asking God to spare me this day. He answered as the landing gear held. Evidently, the problem was that it said in the cabin that the gear wasn't locked in place, but it was. We were OK.

What took place next ranks among one of the nicest things anyone has ever done for me. I had originally had about a three-hour layover in Minneapolis, but now we were down to about an hour before the flight was to leave. I had no idea what I would do, when out of the crowd, John Schwann from Aberdeen asked me if I would be interested in a charter from here to Minneapolis. He said that he and three of his associates absolutely had to be there in an hour, so he asked if I would share the cost of a charter. This was great news as I didn't have to worry about how to make different arrangements for all my connections.

There was only one plane available for charter, and it would hold six people, including the pilot. The problem was we could not take much luggage as we would be overweight. This was once again like the baggage issue with the Alaskan trip but with a different ending. This time the pilot insisted that we stay within our weight, which left this choice: if all five people would go, the only luggage we could take was about 120 pounds. If I would go, I couldn't leave part of my hunting gear home, and I had about 120 pounds. Therefore, John and his friends decided that all five of us would go, and they would leave their luggage at the airport so I could take all of mine. Have you ever heard of a nicer story than this? The second part here is also as good. I told John I didn't have any way of paying my share of the charter. He said, "That's OK. You can pay me when you get home from Alberta." Wow, what a nice guy!

We made it to Minneapolis in time for me to make the flight to Edmonton. It was a short night, and I was up early to catch the bus to Grande Cache. I was a little sleepy as we left the bus station, so I was not paying much attention to the driver of the bus. What I started to notice as we were stopping at quite a few stoplights was the suddenness of each stop. It seemed like the driver was hitting the brakes awfully hard, and we sort of lunged forward each time. Then upon leaving the light, the diesel sounded like it was working overtime. This continued for about five or so miles. We finally got out of town, and the motor still seemed to be laboring.

We own quite a few trucks for our farming operation, and I was thinking that the driver had left the parking brakes on. It really made sense, the way the bus was acting. We hadn't gone more than another few miles when I looked out my window and saw flames coming out from the area where the rear tires were. I looked at the driver, and I thought he saw the flames in his rearview mirror, but I was convinced he had no idea the bus was on fire. I was sure only moments passed here, but it seemed much longer, and I decided I had to do something. I jumped from my seat and headed to the front, startled the driver as I tapped his shoulder, and told him he had better look in his mirror. Then he asked me what he should do with the bus. I told him he had to get off the road so we could get out and, hopefully, get the luggage from the bottom before it went up in flames. I was being a little selfish here as I didn't want to lose my stuff, but who wouldn't be?

What the driver did next was unbelievable. He pulled off the road, and it just so happened we were in a little town that had a gas station right along the road. He pulled into the station and parked the burning bus right next to the gas pumps. You know it; I said aloud to him, "YOU'VE GOT TO BE KIDDING." Then I said, "Get this flipping bus away from the pumps and pull it to that open area." I pointed to a corner about one hundred feet away. Everyone hurriedly got off, I opened the luggage doors, and we all scrambled to get our bags. I was so thankful to get all of mine. There was a home located fairly close but far enough away to be relatively safe. Then I spotted a water hose on a reel that was begging me to take it and try to put the fire out.

What I did next was really stupid. I was putting water on the flames, but I was standing too close to the bus. The next thing I knew was a loud *kaboom* as one of the tires right in front of me blew up. I had pieces of burning rubber and wire hitting me like shrapnel. It must be my lucky day, and I escaped with only a few minor cuts. By this time, the local fire department had showed up, and they continued my work. They were smart enough to do it from quite a distance away. We got the fire out, and then we waited as the driver called his dispatcher. He worked to line up another bus to come out of Edmonton and pick us up. It was really funny as I listened to the conversation. The driver said he had no idea what could have caused the fire to start. He mumbled something about a cigarette. I looked away smiling, not saying a word.

The new bus arrived, and luckily, we got to keep the new driver. The rest of the trip to Grande Cache went great, and Gary, the outfitter, was there to meet me at the end of it. After the introductions, I related the incredible experience the trip had been thus far. I called it the crash and burn, and he laughed. Gary had very kind eyes, and he assured me that everything going forward would be fantastic. I just love that kind of optimism in people as I'm the same way. Something really has to fail miserably for me to admit that it isn't working. We picked up a few supplies and then started the ride out to the base camp. It was raining a little, but I didn't mind as I really was thrilled to be here. We were on horseback, and it took about a four-hour ride to reach the camp. We were on the banks of the big Smoky River.

This camp, like the rest I'd been in, was very comfortable, and we enjoyed a great meal of moose roast. Gary said the plan was to cross the big Smoky in the morning with the horses and to hunt for twelve days in the Willmore Wilderness area. I had had a great experience with horses last year, so I was looking to use them again; they made the trek so easygoing. Before supper, we headed to the shooting range to check my rifle. I didn't know how, but on my first shot, the scope came back and cut my nose very badly. I was so embarrassed. This had never happened to me, and I couldn't stop the bleeding. This cut was actually a problem during the entire ten days of the hunt. It just wouldn't heal because I was always hitting or scratching it.

It was raining very hard as the generator shut down for the night, and it continued to rain all night with periods of extreme downpours. This kept me awake most of the night. Well, okay, the excitement of the sheep hunt probably had the most to do with my sleeplessness too. In the morning, Gary came with the bad news. It had rained so much that the plans had changed.

Overnight, the big Smoky River had gone from a big river to a torrent that Gary explained cannot be traversed at all with the horses.

My horseback hunt had now become a ten-day backpack hunt. I didn't say the words last night when I cut my nose, but now I couldn't hold back and expel the "YOU'VE GOT TO BE KIDDING." I thanked God that I actually made a very good effort to get in shape again, just as in the Alaska hunt. You have no idea how hard this was for me to do. I like to eat and come from a long line of big eaters. I had to combine very intense running and some sort of low-carb dieting to maintain my weight. Even so, I was not sure if I could survive a ten-day backpack hunt.

Gary had a small rowboat that held two people, and we loaded up to cross the raging river. The boat was only big enough to take my guide, Dale Printup, and myself across but with no gear. We headed across, and the current was unbelievable, so consequently, by the time we hit the other side, we had traveled more than a mile downstream. I unloaded, and Dale said he would cross back to the other side, he would haul the boat on his back up the riverbank, and then he would be back with some of our gear. Now here I was with nothing but my rifle, and it looked to me that the trip he was facing would be an all-day affair.

The Big Smokey River looking into the Wilmore Wilderness

It turned into exactly that as by the time he got all our necessary gear across, we only had time to walk a few miles before making camp in the dark.

In the morning, we headed up the mountain as we needed to get above tree line. We camped again that evening in the two-man tent we were carrying with us. I smelled so bad from perspiring, and it was only day 2. I couldn't imagine sleeping in this condition for possibly the next week or more. I only had one change of underwear and one extra shirt and pants in my backpack as I was helping Dale carry the food and supplies we needed for our extended stay. Dale said we were about halfway to the area where we would find bighorn sheep. I was certainly glad I had slimmed down a few pounds and could see that if we were to continue the level of exertion we did today, I would be in wonderful condition at the end of the ten days.

The scenery was incredible, and the rain stayed away. As day 2 ended, we had reached an altitude and area where we could begin the hunt. We were camped at tree line and would hunt up and along the ridgelines to try to find a suitable ram. The weather had turned colder, and the wind was blowing. It looked like in the morning, we would have snow. As I left South Dakota to begin this hunt, I was, as usual, very optimistic that I could harvest a very good ram. Now the way things had progressed, I was unsure of what exactly to expect. I know that in sheep hunting, it usually is necessary to cover a lot of country, and without the horses, we were a bit handicapped. The other factor was it had taken us three days to reach the hunt area, whereas with the horses, we would have been here in one day, thus reducing my hunting time by two whole days. However, I put the pessimistic thoughts out of mind as all we had to do was pick the right direction to go when we left the camp in the morning. I had faith that Dale would go the right way.

We woke to about six inches of snow, and Dale said that it would be to our advantage as it makes the rams easier to see when we glass the mountains above the tree line. I guess the rams stay mostly in the trees but come out to feed on the sparse grass located on the rocky peaks. We spent the next three days climbing peaks so as to look into new valleys. We were not seeing many animals, but we kept up our optimism. The next two days, we went a little different angle from the camp, and we started seeing sheep. It seemed like the trees were thicker and greener. I'm not sure if this was to our advantage, but our numbers were up. On day 6 of our actual hunt, day 9 since we had left the base camp, Dale spotted a group of eight rams. We had had a conversation the previous evening about how long we could actually stay on the mountain. Dale thought if we hunted two more days, that would be it, so seeing these rams got me extremely excited.

Bighorn habitat

They were located near the top of a ridge we estimated to be about two miles away. One of the rams appeared to be what we sought, so we started after them. We spent five hours climbing, side hilling to get above and downwind of them. We crossed over the top and got ready for a shot. The rams were in their beds, and the biggest one was out of sight except for his horns. We waited for almost two hours with our faces into the wind before they stood to eat. I was chilled, but I warmed very quickly with the chance of taking my ram. One shot, and he was down. However, he didn't stay. The reason we hadn't been able to see his body while he was sleeping was that he was down in a very steep creek bed. After the shot, he went down and then proceeded to roll down the creek bed. Dale and I could only watch, and I hoped his horns and hide would be OK. It seemed like forever, but he appeared to stop finally. We started down after him and found out why he had rolled so easily. We were slipping and falling all the way to him. It was a real shale slide, and every step of the way was a challenge not to go the way of my ram, rolling down forever.

Number three of the "Grand Slam"

I was so thrilled to have taken my ram. I now had the three-quarter Slam. After a prayer of thanks and some high fives, we looked for a place to tie the ram to hold him from going farther down, so we hooked him around a rock. Even with this setup, we had a challenge in getting the skinning done. The picture taking was not easy as we kept thinking he might start to roll again. We spent the best of four hours getting pictures, skinning, and deboning all the meat. We then headed out with overloaded packs to the camp. We tried to take a shorter route back, but that meant crossing two major canyons. We got back to our tent at 2:30 a.m. Thank God for giving us a clear sky, so we had the light of a full moon to traverse the rocky conditions.

We didn't rise too early the next morning, but when we did, we spent a little time getting the camp packed. My dilemma was now there were the horns, the full hide, and all the meat to bring with us.

Packing out the ram along with the camp

What I did next really amused Dale. I took a garbage bag, put all my clothes in it except what I was wearing, and tied it up in a tree about twelve feet above the ground. He laughed, and I said to bring my clothes out with them if they ever came this way with horses sometime in the future. Three years later, I got a UPS package with my stuff.

The trip back to the camp was a little easier only because it was downhill. We had really heavy packs, probably 120 pounds each. I was exhausted the first night, but I couldn't have cared less. I had met the challenge and received my prize. We made it to the crossing of the big Smoky River the following evening. The water had gone down, and the raft was waiting for us. Dale crossed over and returned with horses to take everything across.

The next day, Gary, the outfitter, and I headed out on the horses to Grande Cache. We stopped by the conservation office and got my sheep horns plugged. He then said he was going back to Edmonton and asked if I wanted to ride with him or take the bus again. You probably know the answer to that question. Thus, I ended my Rocky Mountain bighorn sheep hunt, and it certainly ended better than it began. I now had my number 8 species.

CHAPTER 6

The Salmon Fisher

It has been three years since my first trip to Alaska. I have never been bear hunting, so to have a trip to Alaska to hunt brown bear meant I was twice as excited. As described in chapter 2, I have been close to grizzly bears, at least the three bears that were after our moose meat. I really was excited then as I watched their antics. I know the hunt I have planned will be incredible as we will also see bears.

It is the end of August 1995, and I am flying to Yakutat, Alaska. Last year, I got my Rocky Mountain bighorn, but I could devise no plan to go after a desert bighorn. I would be thrilled to finish my grand slam. There is still some talk of Mexico opening up again, but no word yet. The only choices for me at this point are the drawings in the southwestern states. I am applying, but the odds of being drawn are very poor, especially when you are a nonresident. Therefore, I decided I would go after a bear. I wanted to return to Alaska, so I thought the Alaskan brown bear would be a good choice.

Once again, John Gates of Blair Worldwide Hunting had a recommendation for me. He suggested I book the hunt with Jungles, Deserts, and Mountains. The owner, Mark Collins, hunts brown bear and wolf, and in the spring, he hunts for glacier bears. He was highly recommended by John because of highly successful fall brown bear hunts. I chose the fall because the spring bear hunts in Alaska happen at the same time as the crop planting window on the farm. Both operations, planting and harvesting, are critical, but there is more forgiveness at harvest. The area Mark hunts in the fall is across Yakutat Bay to the west from Yakutat, Alaska. We will be right next to the world-famous Hubbard Glacier. The hunting here is spectacular because you are hunting low-lying plains right next to the ocean. The streams are full of salmon this time of year, so consequently, there are very large numbers of bears that have access to greater numbers of salmon.

My good friend Larry Brandenburg will accompany me on this hunt. He has not been bear hunting either, so it will be a learning experience for us both. Larry lives in Seattle, so the plan is to meet there and then fly to Yakutat the next morning. Larry picks me up at the airport and proceeds to tell me he has a big surprise. Okay, I have no idea what he is about to spring on me as he can be quite the prankster at times. I join him for supper, and Larry introduces his girlfriend, Janelle. After we finish our meal, I got what I would call more than a surprise from Larry; it was more like a bomb. It seems Larry had been in contact with Mark Collins and had arranged to have Janelle go to the bear camp with him. Already, I'm only partway into this hunt, and I'm thinking, YOU'VE GOT TO BE KIDDING. Now I know it probably isn't such a big deal, but it rubs me the wrong way. Maybe it's because it is a surprise, and he didn't ask what I thought. Janelle is a very nice person, and it appears that she can handle the outdoor part of hunt. It's just that I thought this was a couple of "buds" going to Alaska to bear hunt.

When we leave Seattle for Yakutat in the morning, however, I'm back to my fun-loving self. I have gotten over Larry's "surprise" and looking forward to a new adventure. I shouldn't have been upset about Janelle as there are many hunters who take their spouse or girlfriend on the hunts. As you will see in the next chapters of this book, Becky was with me on a few hunts. The scenery outside my airplane window for the majority of the flight into Yakutat is every bit as good as it was approaching Anchorage. The Canadian Rockies are indeed very rugged. All the high valleys are filled with glaciers. I can't wait to see an up close view of Hubbard Glacier. According to Mark, our outfitter, we will be hunting close enough to hear it calving.

Mark met us at the airport, and after the usual small talk, we head up town to pick up a few supplies. We drive by the pier where the local fishing boats are moored. They are twenty-five below the top of the pier. I think how odd that they would build the pier so high. However, when I ask Mark about it, he just laughs and says, "I guess you haven't heard about the huge tides we have here." Evidently, twice a day, there are twenty-five-foot changes in the sea level. I really felt embarrassed that I didn't know about the tides. Oh well, I don't get off the farm near often enough.

Actually, these tides play a role in producing quite a phenomenon that we would see later as we hunted for bears. In lots of places quite close to the ocean, we would find huge rocks lying in the flattest places. They were too far from the mountains to have broken off and rolled. What happens is as the Hubbard Glacier calves, the big chunks of ice contain these big rocks. Now with the huge tides, they are carried from the glacier out to the sea, and the wind blows the icebergs up the shallow creeks. The ice melts, and there, you have huge rocks in the wrong place. They can never go anywhere as they are now grounded.

Looking across Yakutat bay to the Hubbard Glacier

As we are getting supplies, Mark remarks that if we want to take any alcohol to the camp, we will have to get it now. He continues and says that after we take the small floatplane across Yakutat Bay to the west and get to the camp, we will be there for eight days. I decide I will take a case of beer so I will have refreshments to celebrate the taking of my bear. Larry and Janelle say they are fine and take nothing. We head back to the airport to catch the floatplane. We are about to learn about Alaska's fickle weather.

Fog has settled over the bay, and the wait is on. We have to stay right at the airport because the Alaska weather is like South Dakota. We have a saying at home we use all the time: "If you don't like the weather, stick around. It will be different in five minutes." It's about 2:30 p.m. when the waiting starts, and it continues until dark. Therefore, we will not make it to the camp today, and so we head uptown to get motel rooms.

The morning brings more of the same. We are all anxious to get going, but the waiting continues. As I said in chapter 1, I am not a patient man, but I try to pass the time by reading. I never really kept track of how many hours or days I spent fogged in during my hunting career, but it would be a substantial amount. After my forty-plus hunts, I actually am 100 percent more patient than I was on this hunt. That's a good thing; it's too bad I didn't learn earlier in my hunting career.

Sometime after lunch, the fog lifts, and we load our gear on the plane. It's interesting that this time, we have no restriction on weight. We are also in luck as the tides are right to land over at the camp. If it were high tide, we would be waiting again at the airport because the plane is actually going to land on the beach of the ocean. Therefore, we could not tolerate high tide as there would be nowhere to land. Luck is working in our favor, and the flight across the bay is phenomenal. There are two big cruise ships up close and personal to the Hubbard Glacier. The backdrop behind the camp is the St. Elias Wilderness area of Canada. I know I have never seen so many rugged peaks in one area. We land and haul our gear from the beach to our new home. The accommodations are perfect with individual rooms for hunters. We have flown today, so the hunt will start in the morning. We spend the afternoon fishing in the stream next to the camp. It has a pretty strong current and is just about over our hip boots when we are in the middle. I hope it never gets any deeper as we have to cross it to hunt. All the bear territory is on the opposite side.

St. Elias Wilderness area behind camp

We catch some pretty nice salmon, and it's easy to see why the bears like the area. We see our first brown bear about two miles from the camp, but it's a female, and we aren't going to take a female unless by mistake. We see a few more bears, which are too small. The greatest event of the day is when we see a gray wolf. I have a wolf tag and try to get a shot off. Mark says it is about two hundred yards away, and if it stops, take the shot. I take the shot, but I miss.

On day number 2, we split up, and Mark takes Larry. Sometime in the afternoon, Mark and Larry run into an eight-foot male, and Larry makes a one-shot kill. I guess the bear stood on his hind legs to get a better look at his pursuers, and Larry let him have it through the heart. He is so excited, and the celebration starts when they get back to the camp that night. He is a little upset that he has only taken an eight-foot bear, but I tell him it is still well above average for brown bears. I know everyone wants a ten-footer, but they are hard to come by.

My day was just all right. I say that even though we saw about

65

five small bears. The day was ruined for me as I shot at three more wolves and missed all three. The guide told me again the distance was about two hundred yards, so I would aim just a little low but missed each time. My Weatherby is sighted for zero at three hundred yards, which makes it a little high at two hundred yards; thus, I was holding a little low. I am not able to figure why I'm missing as I'm usually a pretty good shot. I took all three of my rams with one shot each.

On day 3, Mark and I hunt together, and we run into a mother bear with three little cubs. She has a salmon in her mouth and is running with the little guys following her, looking for a meal. Also, later in the day, we come around a corner in a stream, and there, not fifty yards away, are two bears. I don't know how they didn't hear us as we were making a lot of noise as we waded in the stream. Anyway, we are downwind, so they can't smell us. It appears to be a sow with a three-year-old. We would be allowed to take either one, but they are too small. We see a few more bears before we head into the camp for the night. Larry and Janelle stayed in the camp and worked on their bear hide. They have made arrangements to have the plane pick them up tomorrow and head back to Seattle.

As day 4 begins, our weather is changing. The temperature is now only about 38 degrees, and a light rain begins to fall. Mark and I head out to hunt, and Larry and Janelle stay and wait for the plane. It's on and off fog, so it doesn't look good for flying. Flying here at Yakutat is so interesting because you work around the tides. After lunch, we get a bit of sun, and another wolf is spotted by Mark. It is so cool as he is fishing salmon in the stream, just as the bears do. The only difference as we watch him is he is so good at catching fish. The bears kind of slap around and hope something jumps in their mouth. Not the wolf. He watches and then goes right in with his mouth and catches salmon. I am ready to get this wolf, and Mark gives the usual two-hundred-yard distance. I ask myself how they all can be at two hundred yards. It looks farther to me as I have to put my Zeiss scope on nine power to see where to put the shot. I decide to assume he is five hundred yards and aim about eight inches over his back. I shoot, and I have my wolf. We step it off as we approach the trophy, and it is, indeed, a little over five hundred yards. I now know why I missed all the other shots.

During the picture taking, I try to lift this wolf. I can barely get it off the ground. Mark estimates it weighs about 150 pounds. I am so happy to get a wolf as this is another species on my list. We see quite a few bears as the day goes on, but none are big enough. We also see another nine wolves. At this point, Mark says to me, "You've seen more wolves than I've seen in almost all the years I've hunted brown bear here. You must be some kind of wolf magnet." Almost as unbelievable as we are nearing the camp, we look back, and two wolves are following us. One is pure black, and I wish I had another tag. At this point, after seeing a total of sixteen wolves and shooting at five of them before I got one, and now to have two following us, I have to say "YOU'VE GOT TO BE KIDDING."

The "salmon fisher"

As we finish the trip to the camp, it is pouring rain. I am glad to get back, but the stream was a real problem to cross this time. We have to get across to get to the camp on the other side. The water level appears to have come up a few inches after just a couple hours of rain. The camp is quiet as Larry and Janelle got their ride back to Yakutat sometime during the day. We get ready for supper, and I'm thirsty and want to celebrate my great trophy wolf and all the sightings of bears and wolves.

I look for my beer, and I find none. "What in the world?" I ask Mark. There have been no visitors to the camp, I haven't had any beer, and Mark doesn't drink, so that leaves only one answer—Larry and Janelle. However, I know Larry doesn't drink beer, so I have narrowed the investigation to one suspect—Janelle. I didn't mention at the start of this story that she and I share the exact same birthday. I like beer, and I guess anyone born on my exact birthday also likes beer.

Consequently, I have no beer, and I am pissed. I say to Mark, "YOU'VE GOT TO BE KIDDING." But as I look at the situation, how mad can I be? I have taken a wonderful trophy, and I mean wonderful as the skull measured sixteen and change, and it went into the SCI record book as number 2; yes, that's right, number 2. I am so blessed and once again thank God for my good fortune. Tomorrow we will concentrate on a big brown bear.

It rains all night, and at daybreak, we see that our stream is now a river. This is day number 5, and we are going nowhere. It's still raining, so that means a day in the camp reading and sleeping. Hunting days numbers 6, 7, and 8 are mirror images of day 5. So my eight-day hunt turns out to be only four days. I think about saying "YOU'VE GOT TO BE KIDDING," but I've used that enough this hunt. I really could have used a nice cold beer during the four days in the cabin though.

I saw a total of thirty-three bears and had chances to take a bear as big as Larry's, but I really wanted something a bit bigger. Little did I know at this point that the brown bear and the black bear would turn out to be so hard for me to collect. As you will learn, I had to go on another three hunts before I would get a brown bear and three hunts more after that before I would get a black bear. The trip back to Yakutat happened on the morning of day 9. How ironic that the sun was shining, and it was a beautiful day.

When I returned home, it was time to harvest kidney beans, corn, and soybeans so I could get the bank paid and try to put a little in the hunt fund for another brown bear hunt.

CHAPTER 7

Buck

What would you think if you had traveled two thousand miles from home to hunt northwestern white-tailed deer and your guide was named Buck? I assumed that a man whose nickname was Buck and was guiding hunters to trophy white-tailed deer would be some sort of guru. I thought his knowledge of the species would surpass anything I had encountered up until now. Buck had many outstanding qualities, and he was a great guy to spend time hunting. He possessed more knowledge of whitetail habits than a person could gather from all the great books written on the subject.

It is not quite daylight on November 15, 1996, and my brother Herb and I find ourselves in tree stands, staring across a very large wheat stubble field near Fort Vermillion, Alberta. We are located on opposite ends of this large field, looking for trophy whitetail. It is -40 degrees Fahrenheit and breezy, and we are freezing our nads off. We arrived at the camp about three o'clock this morning and got a few hours of sleep before climbing into these iceboxes. When we booked this hunt, I am sure there was mention about heated tree stands. Maybe they meant during the summer months, they are heated by the sun. The only heat here this morning is what our bodies are producing, and that is very shy of being enough.

Yesterday proved to be a very event-filled day. We left South Dakota early in the morning for the flights to Edmonton, Alberta. It is almost becoming routine for me to have trouble getting to hunting camps in Canada because of airline problems. Yesterday offered nothing new as the direct flight from Minneapolis to Edmonton changed to a flight from Minneapolis to Calgary and then Edmonton. The wait at Canadian customs in Calgary was so long we missed the flight to Edmonton. We did get there about five hours later than the original plan. Charlie Stricker was the outfitter for this hunt; his representative had a very long wait at the airport in Edmonton.

Finally, we met Chris and loaded our gear into his older two-wheel-drive, single-cab Chevrolet pickup. He told us we had a five-hour trip north to the hunting camp near Fort Vermillion, Alberta. When we left Edmonton, the temperature was a beautiful -35 degrees Fahrenheit. We were excited, and as we talked about our hunting experiences, we didn't notice how cold it was inside the truck until fifteen minutes later. We were informed that the heater didn't work very well. We had just enough warmth to keep a little area on the front windshield clear to be able to see outside. The road was mostly ice with a light covering of snow, thus making the choice of a two-wheel-drive pickup kind of crazy for this trip.

We are traveling about 45 mph with no heat, and I say the five-hour trip is likely to be closer to eight hours. The combination of these two items caused the first "YOU'VE GOT TO BE KIDDING" moment for this hunt. What's really crazy about this story is that neither my brother nor I thought about having Chris stop the truck so we could get our warm hunting clothes from our bags in the back and put them on to stay warm. How this would escape our thinking for over six hours remains a mystery to this day.

It is now 2:00 a.m., and our young driver is lost. He has never been to the camp before. We have been traveling a series of roads back and forth in the country, looking for the farmhouse that is to serve as the camp. The roads all look alike as they are laid out in mile grids, and the country is very flat. We are looking at the real possibility of having to wait until daylight to find our site. But at 3:00 a.m., out of sheer luck, we arrive at the house. Next, we have a long search for a key to get inside, and then we can't start the furnace, and so ends our day. When we awaken at 5:00 a.m., we learn our young driver had stayed up long enough to fix the furnace so we at least had a warm house.

After making sure we have everything in our packs for the morning hunt, we leave, and a new search in the dark begins to find Buck's house. The good news is he lives close by, and we find him relatively easily. We knock on the door and waken him; as he gets dressed, we wait outside in the cold truck. Buck comes out of the house carrying a battery and proceeds to put it in his little red truck. What? We learn this is how Buck plugs his truck in so it will start when it is negative forty below. He has no block heater in the vehicle, which seems insane when living in the far north.

So after a short chat about the weather, Buck says for me to put my stuff in his truck. We load ourselves into the truck, and I just have to break out in laughter at the next two things that happen. I'm sure Buck was wondering why it's so funny, but he hadn't had the experiences we've had the last twenty-four hours. First, a screwdriver appears in Buck's hand, and he pushes it into the keyslot to start the vehicle. He turns it, and the vehicle immediately lurches forward and heads down the hill by his house. I hear the engine start, and away we go. I look at him while laughing, and I realize that the key switch is broke; thus, the screwdriver and the clutch is also out, thus the trip down the hill.

Now I'm with Buck headed for my tree stand, and Herb is with Chris headed for his stand in the two-wheel-drive truck with no heater. Whew! What a start to this hunt. No, I'm not going to say it. Okay, I changed my mind. "YOU'VE GOT TO BE KIDDING."

I am not prepared for long periods in a tree stand at -40 degrees, so Buck says he will come back to pick me up in a few hours. You really have to have some faith in God that Buck and his truck will actually be capable of retrieving me. I am also thinking of Herb as there is quite a bit of snow on the trails to get into this field. I don't think the two-wheel drive can make it down the trails without getting stuck. At this point, I can only picture Herb and I both walking wherever we need to go on this hunt. Now how could I get pessimistic on the first morning of the hunt?

Buck is a farmer, so we have lots to talk about. We are hunting some of his fields and some of his neighbor's. The whitetails are rutting, so the plan is to sit in the stands for a few hours in the morning and then a few hours again in the evening. During the day, Buck drives me around, and we search fields and small areas of trees for trophy bucks. During the drive around on day number 2, we run into a very nice Canadian moose. Buck has a license for moose but only owns a .22 rifle. So he is looking at me and my .300 Weatherby, and he asks me to shoot that moose for him. I say to him, "Let's analyze this scenario. I am in a foreign country and would be hunting and shooting an animal without a license, so the answer is absolutely not." I think he is actually hurt by my refusal, but what else could I say?

"Buck's" truck, No key switch, clutch, or block heater

The number of deer we see is fewer than expected, but Buck says this is the very northernmost boundary for whitetail, so their numbers are quite low. I have seen more deer than Herb has, but I don't think they can get to all the places we can. Once Buck gets the vehicle going in the morning, we really do cover some territory. The morning of day number 5 produces nothing from the stand, but it has warmed up to only be about -10 degrees. It is overcast, and Buck says a storm is coming, so the deer will be moving around more. Sometime around noon, his theory seems to be working as we do see more deer. We are driving down a farm road and hit a dead end. As we stop, Buck excitedly points out to the middle of the 160 acres of wheat stubble in front of us. A quick look with the binoculars reveals two deer lying in the field. One is a doe, and the other is a very big buck. I ask Buck how far. He says, "What difference does it make? Let's just get back in the truck as we are going to get going." I ask where we're going. He says we are going to chase after the deer with the truck. I say, "What do you mean chase after the deer?" "Well, yeah," he says, "we chase after them and get close, and you shoot out the window."

To me, this sounds ridiculous, and I say, "YOU'VE GOT TO BE KIDDING." I tell Buck, "I'm sure this is just as illegal as the moose you wanted me to shoot!" All right now, we need plan B. I say, "What about the idea that these deer are not spooked and we get ready for a shot if they stand?" Buck says he thinks it will be about 350 yards, and I agree with that. I can make a 350-yard shot at a standing target much easier than the rifle out the window at 35 mph. My rifle is zeroed at 300 yards, so I will hold a few inches high if I get a shot. This is not my first whitetail hunt as I have hunted them for twenty years around the farm, though I have never had a chance at a really big deer like the one I am currently looking at.

As we wait for the deer to stand, I thank God for the good fortune for having put us here at this time. The usual thoughts of making a good shot are rolling around in my mind. I look at Buck, and he says he has never hunted like this before. The longer we wait, the harder it becomes to stand with the rifle on ready while the cool wind blows in our face. Finally, the deer stand and present a broadside shot. I take the shot, and the buck collapses. I wished I had the camera in my hand instead of the rifle at that moment so I could capture the look of awe on Buck's face. I was feeling pretty cocky, so I said, "Well, what do you think of that?" I would have looked really stupid if the buck had gotten up and run away while I was bragging myself up.

This scenario really adds a new meaning to the phrase "buck fever." I will forever think of Buck while preparing for a shot at a whitetail.

The buck that put the look of dis-belief on "Buck's" face

My best whitetail

After giving thanks to God, we take our pictures and head for camp. The buck scores 160 plus, so I am extremely happy. Buck is a thrill to hunt with and is full of knowledge about the farm economy in Canada. Brother Herb is unsuccessful this time, and I think it had some to do with the inability to get around the country.

I haven't spent much time hunting whitetail over the years because the hunting fund couldn't stand doing the other species in North America as well as a whitetail hunt occasionally. I did go to British Columbia with a couple of friends and hunt with Gary Drinkall a few years later. I got a deer just a little bigger than 161 and was so glad that Gary's stands were actually heated. I didn't get the deer from the stand, but my guide, Justin Keutzer, and I actually spent time hunting deer the old-fashioned way, which is stalking on foot. He was a very good hunter, and I was pleased that he knew some of the deer habits.

The whitetail I got with Buck puts my total species taken to date at ten.

The world famous "BUCK" with my great whitetail

CHAPTER 8

Pure Luck

There should be a time in a person's life where good luck abounds every now and then. This trip to Sonora, Mexico, to hunt Coues deer was one of the luckiest weeks I've had in my short life. It is December 1996, and I am in Sonora, Mexico, hunting with Ramon Campillo of Campillo Brothers outfitting. My goal is to take another species of North American animal, a Coues white-tailed deer. To date, with the northwestern whitetail I got last year in Alberta, I now have ten species, and this will make number 11.

Concerning my hunting, I am now at a crossroads and almost think of the possibility of completing the North American 29 daily. I am a perfectionist by nature, and once I start a project, I have to see it to conclusion. Before choosing to continue to pursue the 29, I ask myself many questions: How would I ever pay for all the hunts? Will my health allow me to finish? If I go hunt, should I hold out for one of every species that will qualify for entry into the record books of trophy animals? If I do hold out for trophy animals, will I have the funds necessary to go on multiple hunts for every species? The answers to these questions varied by the day.

After much thought, I decided that my goal for animal size would be, first, to take only males and, second, for them to be at least better than average size. The ten animals I have taken so far all qualified for SCI's record book. I wanted to continue to strive for quality animals, and you'll see as the chapters unfold that I indeed got better than average size and I did hold out for the record book. I guess that as time progressed, I was not so concerned about the record book, but I really had a lot of good fortune on most of my hunts.

Okay, on to the story of the Coues deer. The hunt was for the middle of December 1996. My flight took me from home in South Dakota to Tucson, Arizona, and then on Aero Mexico to Hermosillo, Sonora. I overnighted in Hermosillo, and Ramon Campillo met me at the hotel about 9:00 a.m. We sat around a table in the entryway and chatted about where we were going and how good the hunting had been to date. I had met Ramon and his brother, Bobby, at the SCI convention back in 1992, where we were introduced by Jeff Blair. They ran two very successful hunting operations in Sonora. Bobby outfitted for desert mule deer, and Ramon did the Coues deer hunts. In another chapter, there will be a story about hunting desert mule deer with Bobby, but these pages belong to Ramon.

After about an hour, we loaded my gear into Ramon's truck, and we headed northeast from Hermosillo. We were going to a private ranch outside Banamichi, Sonora. The way Ramon described the ranch, it sounded huge. I was really excited by all the stories of the big deer they had taken over the years. I was told this ranch actually received very little hunting pressure and that they actually kept some ranch hands on the payroll just to police against poachers. I think the outfitters in Mexico who are successful have to control the poachers, or their quality of animals goes down very quickly.

We are about an hour away from Hermosillo, and Ramon says we might as well do our paperwork before we reach the ranch. I said sure as I had the money for the hunt in cash in my wallet. The total I owed was $3,500 for the seven-day hunt. I reached for my wallet and immediately went into panic mode. My wallet was not in my pocket. We pulled over, and the search began. I checked all my bags and nothing.

Then it registered in my thoughts that I had left it on the table in the hotel lobby where we had been talking earlier in the day. I was going to pay Ramon then, and I had taken it out of my pocket, but I was so excited seeing all the pictures of big trophy deer they were showing me that I left it lying on the table when I left. Now Ramon gave me the bad news when he said, "There is no use in going back as it will be long gone." You know, that is not exactly what I was hoping to hear. At this point, I really had no idea how I would pay Ramon. I suggested that we should go back, and I would cover the cost of the gas. I guess Ramon's puzzled look came from the fact that I had no money, so how was I going to buy gas?

I must have been persuasive enough because we turned around and went back. We arrived at the hotel and learned that some God-fearing soul had turned my wallet into the desk clerk. Everything was still there, including about $4,500 cash. All I could say after thanking God was "YOU'VE GOT TO BE KIDDING." I think all this really surprised Ramon, but he was just as happy as I was. After leaving a nice tip for the clerk and the saint who turned my wallet, we were once again on our way. I immediately handed Ramon his $3,500 so he could worry about it and not me. This is not the first time I have lost my wallet, and it always seems to happen when I have large amounts of cash in it. My wife says I really need to have the chain, but I haven't felt I fit the description of those with the chain-drive wallets.

Our arrival at the camp was obviously after dark because of my carelessness. The accommodations were perfect, and the rest of the hunters were very cordial and only teased me a little about my stupidity. One of the group said I was pretty lucky as it may not have turned out so well if I had done that in some parts of the United States. The fact that we got in after dark will prove to be a major detriment a little later in this story. I met my guide, José, who speaks no English, but from what I learn, he is one of their best guides. His technique for finding the big deer went outside the normal for Coues deer hunting. It seems José spends all day walking or climbing the mountains. He jumps the deer from their bedding grounds instead of gaining elevation and glassing for hours at great distances to locate the big deer. I was coupled with José as the camp director, David May, who is also a sheep hunter, thought I was in the best sheep shape of the hunters who were in the camp this week. You know, I really like José's approach to hunting as I love to walk and climb versus to sit all day and glass. I really feel lucky to have José.

We leave the camp in the dark. We are traveling in an old Chevy blazer, and José and I have a driver. I guess the scenario is the driver is going to take us quite far this morning. Before we begin to hunt, the driver and José will formulate a plan whereby the driver will pick us up later in the day. I guess this all fits with José's style of hunting.

We are about an hour from the camp when we hear a tire blow on the rear of the blazer. We get all the gear out to change the tire, but we are missing the handle to run the hydraulic jack up and down. I just smile and say to the driver that it'll be a long walk back to the camp. I'm thinking José and I could just hunt our way back, but we've been driving through a ranch we can't hunt.

As a farmer, there are many times we have to improvise when it comes to tools, so I scour the blazer for anything that will work in the jack. We just need something about an inch in diameter and four to five inches long, although a little longer would also work. Try as we might, we have nothing that will work. I sit and want to get a diet Pepsi from my backpack. I am a diet Pepsi fanatic by the way, and I try to have at least a couple fifty-two-ounce cups per day. Anyway, as I am looking in the pack for my bad habit, I spot at my small Maglite flashlight. It's about the right diameter and length for a jack handle. I pull it out, insert it in the jack, and proceed to raise the vehicle. Of course, José smiles, and I say, "YOU'VE GOT TO BE KIDDING." What a great commercial this would be for Maglite flashlights. I really had no idea they were that tough, but it sure was a lifesaver. José and my driver are high-fiving. How lucky is this for the first morning?

We continue in the blazer for about another mile or so, and the hunt begins. The first day, we spend most of the day climbing some very steep mountains, and I quickly learn why they call a good Coues deer hunt a poor man's sheep hunt.

We see some deer but nothing big enough. I am really impressed with José as he somehow seems to know where the deer are and goes right at them. We jump bucks three different times this first day, but they aren't big enough.

The next day, we leave the camp a bit earlier so we can get to the top of a pretty tall peak before daylight. As dawn approaches, we see bucks on the horizon. José is yelling something about *muy grande*, so I try to get the scope on the biggest one. I shoot but appear to miss, so I shoot repeatedly. I stare in disbelief as the deer head down the deep canyon where we quickly lose sight of them. I think I missed because they were too close, and I was shooting over their backs. I can tell José is not pleased, and I am not much happier.

After lunch that day, we jump a really nice buck, and I shoot again and miss. This scenario plays out again later in the day with another miss. I return to the camp that evening pretty humble. I don't know how I could have missed all those shots. I guess every hunter will have buck fever sometime, but I didn't believe this was the case for me. David May, after hearing the stories, suggested I stay in the camp until after daylight tomorrow and check my rifle.

The large Coues' deer inhabit some bighorn sheep-like mountains

At first light, I shoot at a target at one hundred yards. After three shots, I'm not even on the paper. I shoot again, aiming at the bottom of about a twenty-inch target, and I just barely touch the very top. So my scope is off seventeen inches, which explains why I was indeed shooting over the backs of the "gray ghosts of the desert." I am lucky that I had brought three boxes of shells with me as it took about a box and a half to get my gun to shoot where it should be hitting the target. Most hunts I usually would bring only two boxes of shells.

All right, problem fixed, so let's go hunting. This is day 3, and we try a different area but don't see even one buck. There are lots of does, and I'm not surprised by the results of the day as typical deer hunting produces "doe days and buck days." Tomorrow will bring a buck day.

We head back to the ranch we hunted the first day, and I am excited as José seems pretty confident today. We don't see much until about 3:00 p.m. when, after climbing a pretty good peak, we jump a buck out of his bed. This guy is huge and by far the biggest we've seen. We are only seventy-five yards away, and I get the scope right on him. I pull the trigger, and nothing happens. I mean, there is no shot. Right away, I think I have left the safety on, but a quick check shows the safety is off. By this time, the deer is out of sight. I shake my head and mumble, "YOU'VE GOT TO BE KIDDING." I don't even want to look at José as I have no explanation. I guess he wouldn't understand the words anyway. I pull the shell from the gun and see that it just didn't fire. The primer has a dent, but the shell didn't work. This is incredible as I just shot thirty of these shells yesterday, and they all worked. I use only factory Weatherby loads and have never had one that didn't work. The rest of the day produces nothing, but José really isn't into the chase as much as he usually is.

Once again, David May says we should stay in the camp until daylight so we can check out the shells. I shoot three at the target, and they work just fine. I'm starting to worry about having enough to finish the hunt the way it's been going. Now this is day 5, and I can tell José has lost that little skip in his step as we head out to hunt. We have this afternoon to hunt and then tomorrow, so I'm hoping he can pull off his magic one more time. Once again, later in the day, we jump a group of three bucks, and they are all very good, with one at least as good as yesterday. I get the scope on him and pull the trigger, and again, like yesterday, nothing happens. I quickly eject and try again but with the same results. As the deer take to the cactus out of sight, I have to say again "YOU'VE GOT TO BE KIDDING." I really don't know what to do.

That evening when we get to the camp, we find that all the other hunters have filled their tags, and the celebration is on around the campfire. José is nowhere to be found, and I don't blame him for not wanting to be seen. I have embarrassed him. I ask David to tell me what's up, and he says that José says I'm too unlucky. He has shown me so many good bucks, and I don't have one yet, so he is quitting. David says to let him cool off overnight and see what the morning brings. I continue to celebrate my fellow hunters' good success.

The camp staff, including Marie who has provided our group with great cuisine, join our party. As she leaves for bed, our group bids her good night. I have the ridiculous thought that because this is my second trip to Mexico, I can speak some Spanish, and I say to her something like "Buenas natches" when I meant to say "Buenas noches." She turned and smiled as I had just told her she had a "good butt" instead of what I thought I said was "good evening." I was so embarrassed.

A disgruntled Jose' and I started here at camp the last afternoon

As the last day of the hunt dawns, I still have no guide as José is walking around the camp in his underwear and slippers with no intention of hunting. Now I'm not going to pass up hunting the last day. As I said earlier, I'm a perfectionist, and I'm going to finish what I started. David says we should try the shells again. We fire at the target, and they all work. I have exactly three shells left out of the sixty that I brought to the hunt. This whole scenario seems unbelievable, but what do you do? By this time, it is lunchtime, and after we eat, I ask David if he could convince José to just take me out the last few hours, right here behind the camp. There have been some sightings of some good bucks right here, so I thought just maybe, the luck would change.

I'm not sure what David said to José, but he is pissed. He puts on his hunting clothes as fast as he can and heads out the door. The mountain behind the camp is quite steep, and José is practically running up it. I'm behind and trying to keep up. It's not very long until I am a long way behind, and at times, I can hardly see him. Another half hour goes by, and I can't keep up the pace I'm going, so I stop for a short rest. I just get sitting when I see José running down toward me and yelling, "Senor! Senor!" He is waving frantically for me to follow him. Therefore, the push is on as I try to get to him. When I do catch up, I am so out of breath I can hardly see what is causing all the excitement. José points down in the canyon to our right, and I see what every Coues hunter loves to see. Below, at about 150 yards and running away, is a group of four absolutely huge bucks. They head up the other side, and I quickly get my scope on them. It's hard to pick out the biggest one as they are all of trophy size. Finally, I make a decision and pull the trigger, and again, nothing happens. Now this is ridiculous, so I quickly eject the shell and get back on the deer with the scope. By this time, they are ready to top out on the ridge, and in a few seconds, they will be gone out of sight. I have the scope on a different buck now, and he looks even bigger than the last one. Now at this point, I couldn't care less about size. I just want a shell to work. I have two left, so I pull the trigger, and bang, it actually works. The buck falls immediately, but I'm not sure how to respond. He is down for good, and I see José about ready to smile

83

for the first time in a few days. I'm elated but fall to the ground in disbelief of the whole situation.

We wait about fifteen minutes before we start across the canyon to look for my prize. I am not even concerned about the size of the buck; I am just so glad to have one. The canyon is a challenge as they are always steeper than they look when you have to cross. As we near the top of the other side and José gets a glimpse of the buck, he appears to be walking on air. I can't yet see, but I can tell by José's hooting and hollering that the buck must meet his approval. When I finally see it, I have to stop. He is unbelievable, and I say my prayer of thanks.

Started at number 9 in SCI records at 121"

We get the pictures done, and José makes a backpack out of the buck. I have never seen this done before, but it sure facilitates getting it down off the mountain. When we get to the camp, there is no guide in the world at this moment in time that is any happier than José. The other hunters are in awe when they see this buck. David looks at it and says it's the biggest they have ever taken. I rethink the events of the week, the missed shots and the bad shells, and then it hits me. It was all a master plan. Even just a few hours ago, if the shell had fired, I would not have gotten this buck. It wasn't until I ejected the bad shell and got the scope on a different buck that the whole plan came together. What I'm trying to say is all the events had to happen the way they did for the result I got. Thank you, God! As to the factory Weatherby shells, I never had even one shell over the next fourteen years that did not work.

The buck scored 121 and change and went into the SCI record book as the ninth largest. How does it get any better than that? It appeared José was pleased with his hunter after all, and I did leave a nice tip, even though he quit on me. Thus, considering the way this chapter started, you can see how the name Pure Luck fits.

Jose' with a more positive outlook

CHAPTER 9

The Slam

John Gates of Blair Worldwide Hunting has become a very good friend. He has worked very hard to earn my business. With all the phone calls back and forth between the two of us talking about hunts and life in general, it was almost natural that we would be friends. I have always enjoyed working with people who do not use high-pressure techniques to make a sale. John fits that description.

I am amazed that he was able to get me to sign the contract for this hunt, given the amount of money involved. I am as surprised, as I think John is, to find myself heading back to Sonora, Mexico. It is February 1997, and I am going on a hunt for desert bighorn sheep. I obviously let my guard down and let John do what he does best, book another hunt for me. He says that Ernesto Zaragoza is the best choice for desert bighorns. Ernesto operates Solimar Hunting Safaris headquartered in Guaymas, Sonora, Mexico, and he covers over a million acres of hunting ground.

It has only been a couple of months since I was in Sonora as you read in the last chapter. I took my Coues deer in December, and I am still feeling good as that hunt was truly pure luck. As John and I talked about hunting desert bighorns, I tried to assess how many sheep were taken last year in Sonora. I learned at last year's SCI convention that the Mexican government had opened their country for desert bighorns. I also learned that the price for the hunt was $50,000. All I could say to that information was "YOU'VE GOT TO BE KIDDING." I just thought that was an outrageous price.

However, during the summer and fall of 1996, as John and I talked, it became apparent that there were many hunters who needed the desert bighorn to finish their grand slam. This, as you know, included me, and as we analyzed the costs, we were sure this would be a supply and demand hunt. The outfitters could command a high price because they could. My strategy of waiting until the second year did not work very well. There were very good rams taken the first year, so the price then went up to $60,000. I thought I had better try to get a hunt booked before the price got even higher. I was equally mad at myself for not trying the first year because with Sonora allowing no hunting for the bighorns for quite a number of years, there were some huge rams taken.

In talking directly with Ernesto, he was very confident that I would take a ram that would score high enough to go into the Boone and Crockett record book. Now once again, that is the kind of optimism I like, and I really felt good about the hunt. I also liked the fact that after I explained to Ernesto that I thought the price was too high, he added a couple of perks to help the whole deal. He said I could come back in the future, at the time of my choosing, and hunt for a desert mule deer free of charge. I would also be able to bring along an observer on the sheep hunt free of charge. I thought this free observer would be great as I then would have someone to film the entire hunt for me.

Now after doing all the paperwork with John, the search began for someone who wanted to go on my hunt and film for me. The problem was the hunt could last for up to thirty days, so the list of people who could be away that long was very short. Becky could not go as our kids had so many school projects and sports to participate in. My brothers could not go, nor any of the rest of my local hunting friends. I was surprised when I was casually visiting with Larry Brandenburg that he said he could go. If you remember from chapter 7, Larry was my friend from Seattle who went along on the brown bear hunt to Yakutat, Alaska. Actually, on that hunt, it turned out to be Larry and his girlfriend, Janelle. The hunt was set. All I had to do was buy Larry an airline ticket from Seattle to Guaymas, Sonora, Mexico, and I would have my film crew.

Now I was so excited to be going on this hunt that I do not remember all the details of how I ended with enough cash to pay the $60,000. Evidently, I got it somehow. I am sure (and I hope my banker is not reading this) I used my farm operating loan to cover most of it. I do remember that I was supposed to have paid the second half sometime about thirty days before the hunt. I could not get the cash on time, and Ernesto was very kind and patient and waited for it. I actually sent him a wire transfer for the remaining balance of $30,000 while I was changing planes at the Denver airport on the way to the hunt. I really cut that deadline way too close as I could have lost my deposit of $30,000 as well as the hunting trip. I found that with most people, if you tell them the truth, they will usually work with you.

I spent two months of pretty intense training to get into "sheep shape" for this hunt. I was again running about six miles a day, just as I had done before the Dall sheep hunt in Alaska in 1992. I had read more than one story about how tough desert sheep could be to hunt because of the steep terrain involved. I was prepared this time unlike when I embarked on the Stone sheep hunt. I was once again down to around 200 pounds, which for me is a great compromise between my fat weight and my ideal "sheep shape" weight of 185 pounds. You are probably thinking that I should just stay in shape all the time and not have to work so hard right before the hunt. Well, that is a good theory, but my mind does not work that way. I cannot pass up good food and absolutely love all sweets.

Slimmed down a little and ready to finish the "Slam"

The trip to Guaymas was very uneventful, and I am now very familiar with the processes involved to get my gun and myself through Mexican customs. I was not worried when I was not met at the airport. I just checked into the prearranged hotel. I knew that my gun would follow when a representative of Solimar Hunting stopped at the airport. The biggest part of the gun permit is done before you leave home. You have to go to the local sheriff and get them to write you a "good-guy letter," which basically says you are not a wanted criminal or on the outs with the local sheriff's department. I had done this letter four times previously, and I was not sure what the sheriff thought about me bothering him so many times for the letter. I always hate to be a burden on people, but this letter has to be done to obtain your gun permit.

After about a three-hour drive from Guaymas, through some beautiful farm country, we arrived at Ernesto's camp. I could not have been more pleasantly surprised. The accommodations were perfect. We were staying at an old-style Mexican hacienda, the kind most people only see in movies. The introductions began, and I almost could not believe this. I had sixteen people at my beck and call.

They were here to assure I was comfortable and help my chance at taking an unbelievable ram in any way possible. I had Ernesto; the head guide, Dee Wooddell; the second guide, Angel; five trackers; a skinner; two camp cooks; two vehicle drivers; a mechanic; a ranch hand who watched for poachers; and last, Juan, who qualified and had done all of the above. To me, this qualified for a "YOU'VE GOT TO BE KIDDING." Juan, who was to be the guide for my hunt, had actually walked sixty miles to come to the camp to help me. Wow, that is commitment. I know very few people in the United States who would do that for a job. You know, actually, I do not know anyone.

I am by nature an excitable person, but these words cannot begin to describe the emotional high I experienced the first night in the camp. The dinner was incredible as we enjoyed some of the biggest and most flavorful shrimp I have ever encountered. Ernesto and his father operate most of the shrimp fishing in Mexico, so it was only right that we enjoy the best of the best. The cooks could have easily made the grade as head chef at any five-star resort. The wines were exquisite, and I thought after a few too many glasses that sleep would come easy. Not so. I was so thrilled to have come this far in my hunting career, and the thoughts of finishing my slam overrode the effects of great wine. Before retiring for bed, Larry and I talked about the differences in big game outfitters. Although we were only a few hours into this hunt, we agreed that Ernesto would rank right at the top of any list.

Even though I got only a few minutes' rest, I was ready to go at first light. As Larry and I enjoyed breakfast, Dee went over the plan for day 1. We would take Angel and a few trackers with us, and Juan and another group were to explore a different mountain. Oh, the joys of having enough help! The reason I say this stems from the fact that I am sure there is not a farm in North America that would say they have enough help to get all their work done.

We drove to the Los Mochis mountain range and began the climb to the top to facilitate glassing the canyons and rock outcroppings for our quarry. I was generally about the third person in our line of ten people, with Larry following us with the camera. The film rolled whether we as the "actors" were ready. I think Larry really liked the job, and we got some great footage. The desert was very thick, almost junglelike in places. In my previous trips to Mexico to hunt in the Sonoran Desert, the plant life was less abundant. On this trip, we are farther south than I had been in the past. The one constant that remained was every plant had thorns or stickers, and I invariably got tangled up with some of them. This time I found out about devil's claw, and my legs had the scars to prove it.

I swear there are two desert plants that are half human. These are jumping cactus and devil's claw. This is the only explanation for me being caught by them. They had to have been moving toward me as I walked.

We spotted quite a few sheep, mostly mothers and babies. With ten people looking in all directions, it would be highly unlikely that very many sheep should escape our gazing. We spent most of the day at the top and, toward evening, began our descent. I couldn't have cared less if we hadn't even seen sheep today as I was still on my emotional high. We covered some miles, but I was okay; as you know, I was in "sheep shape." During the day, Juan and his group had set up a camp at the bottom. This way, we did not have a long drive back to the ranch and could start earlier tomorrow. The spike camp was almost as good as the base camp, but I did not expect any less from Ernesto.

Myself and part of my army looking for sheep

The next three days were pretty much carbon copies of day 1. We would make a pretty significant climb right away in the morning and spend time glassing and then moving and repeating. It was nice having Dee as head guide as his English was perfect. This made the hunt go so much easier. You will remember in the last chapter that José spoke no English, so after a week, I had gotten very tired of talking to myself. Conversing with Dee, I had time to find out that the entire crew had had years of experience guiding hunters. This made me feel very confident in our search for the above-average ram.

Day number 5 started as usual, but two things occurred, making it stand out. As we returned to the camp in the evening, we learned that Juan and his group had spotted some rams in a different part of the hunt area, and they thought we should move there tomorrow. I was all for this. Next, Ernesto said he had to return to Guaymas for business, and I told him I was fine with this as his help was more than capable. Then the shocker. Larry had decided he was going to ride back with Ernesto and was leaving me. He said he would leave his camera, and one of the trackers could do the filming. I just smiled, did not say a word, and thought to myself, YOU'VE GOT TO BE

KIDDING. I am sure it is very different when the animal you are hunting is not yours personally and that at some point, you have had enough of the wilderness experience. Therefore, with Larry gone, Phillip became the film master. Dee spent an hour explaining the camera's operation, but Phillip and technology did not mix, and the next days' filming produced a blank tape.

Day number 6 was a beautiful day as most of them were while hunting in Sonora. In five hunting trips and over forty days of field time in Sonora, I have yet to see any rain and only one day of wind. We began the day as usual with a climb toward the top of a mountain. The difference today was this was a real mountain, and my "sheep shape" was put to the ultimate test. I was a little embarrassed as I was forty-four years old and I could not climb as well as Juan, who was approaching seventy. However, let's get real; he just walked sixty miles to work. How was I to compete with that? I was at least as capable as Dee, the master guide. He was struggling also, but he did not let that dampen the spirits of our entire group.

We needed to get to the top as the rams were on the far side, and so we pushed hard. About 11:00 a.m., after five hours of climbing, we were in a position to see the country where Juan had spotted the rams. We glassed about an hour, when Angel, who was not using binoculars, spotted the ram. He was about halfway down to the desert floor and moving out. He moved as if something had spooked him. Dee did not think it was our group but quite possibly a mountain lion. This put the ram out of reach. There was no chance to even attempt a stalk. If he stopped his descent while we were above him, we would have the advantage.

We set up the spotting scope, and when I saw him, I began to shake. He was an exceptional ram, and Dee said that he was as big as any they had seen. I could not help but notice the red coloring of his horns. Dee said they were red because the ram had been reaching the inside of a desert tree, and the sap colored the horns red. Juan was excited as this was the ram he had spotted yesterday. As we watched, the ram made a rather hasty descent to the bottom of the mountain and, in a matter of twenty minutes, was all the way down, and we could see him heading across the desert floor.

I must have looked very disappointed because immediately, Dee came to me and said not to worry as he was doing exactly as they wanted and we would get him. I looked at him and said, "OK, you know I have complete faith in you guys." I asked Dee where he thought the ram wanted to go. All I could see was the very vast sea of densely overgrown desert. I knew after my experiences hunting desert mule deer in Sonora that these plants literally swallow up animals, and you never saw them again. Dee answered that he will probably head for another mountain range. OK, again, the look of disappointment. I asked how far to the closest one. Dee said about seven miles.

Now being the eternal optimist that I am, I said, "We know he is going to some new mountain range, but we do not know which, and it is a minimum of seven miles away. We also do not know the route he will take or how long it will take him to get there, but he is doing what we want." Now you know at this point I have to be thinking, YOU'VE GOT TO BE KIDDING. The next statement from Dee made me laugh, and I apologized for laughing, but he said that Angel and the trackers would follow him across the sea of desert, we would follow Angel, and we would find the ram. I could see he was not kidding, and I had to have faith in their plan.

Seven miles of desert and the "ram" mountain

The series of events that took place over the next five or six hours would remain as the number 1 stalk I had ever seen to harvest a wild animal. We began with a descent down the mountain, trying to follow the path the ram used when descending. We moved very quickly, and I was falling more than climbing down. I sincerely hoped my camera operator was getting some footage today, although this was not my main concern. As we neared the bottom, Angel began a very thorough search back and forth to locate the ram's tracks. I watched him demonstrating his skill in amazement. I thought at one point he was about to give up looking, but he was persistent. It was very rocky, mixed with a little sand. When you and I think of a track, we think we will see a complete hoofprint and then the next and so on. But the normal for Angel was finding little pieces of either rock or sand that might be ever so slightly moved. Thank God, I was not the tracker. When Angel announced in his quiet voice that he had indeed found the ram's footprint, I was staring at nothing but small pebbles on the ground.

During the next half hour, Angel followed the ram into the jungle of desert plants. He assured us that he was indeed on the right course. I was just following as I never did see any kind of sign that I could have used to determine the ram's general direction. We followed Angel for another hour, and by now, we were quite some distance from the mountain we had descended. Angel spoke to Dee and pointed to another mountain in the distance. It appeared that the consensus among the group was that the ram was headed exactly where Dee said he would go, that being the location about seven miles away. We were probably still five miles away, but the pace of our trek picked up, with Angel checking the ground briefly every few minutes.

We covered the distance to the base of the mountain, and then the next YOU'VE GOT TO BE KIDDING happened. Dee told Angel he was on the ram's track and that he recommended we circle the mountain with the vehicle. He would be looking for a track, leaving this mountain, and if none was found, we could be sure the ram stayed here. I think you get a sense of my hesitation toward this plan, but how could I question it if I never did see the track? I did have one question for Dee, and I asked if we did find a track around the base of the mountain, how would we know if it was the same ram? Dee said there would be quite a few different tracks back and forth around the base, but we would know our ram because he was leaving a "crooked track." "What?" I said in amazement. Now Dee and Angel had determined that not only were we tracking this ram by prints I had not seen, but also, he had now become "Old Crooked-Foot." You thought I was going to say it, didn't you?

Therefore, off we went with two vehicles. Angel was in the lead vehicle, seated on the right side and was looking out on the ground as we drove. We spent a little over an hour completing the base drive, with Angel getting out only twice. Outside of the vehicle, he would make little circles and climb back aboard. It was a very fast pace as I estimated it to be seven or eight miles around. It appeared that Angel was convinced the ram had stayed here. Now I had another question for Dee. What if, after we drove by, the ram left? He replied we would get on his track again in the morning and find him. "OK," I said, and I thought, *Enough with all my pessimism as I am working here with true professionals.*

We ended where we started the drive around the base, which was the place where the track started up the steep mountain. I was absolutely amazed at how easily Angel got us back to this point as most of the desert looked the same. We got out, and Dee said to get my pack loaded with whatever I would need for a trip up the mountain to take the ram. He said, "Make sure you have your camera." Now that was optimism. So the climb began with Angel leading the way and again following the ram's trail. I did not even bother to look down but instead focused on looking up to see if somehow I could be useful in helping locate the ram. I thought for a group this large, we were very quiet. No one spoke a word, and except for an occasional slip on a rock, there were no sounds. We had spent less than forty-five minutes climbing when Angel and Dee began whispering very quietly. Dee came to me and whispered, "Angel has a feeling and thinks we are very close." I did not even ask for the details of the "feeling" as I have experienced this in many situations.

Everyone having that we are getting close feeling

In less than fifteen minutes, I saw Angel getting all excited and pointing up the mountain. At that point, everyone trained their binoculars on the mountainside and found the ram. He was bedded next to an organ pipe cactus. This was absolutely incredible, finding this ram again. There was no time to waste. I asked Dee what he thought about yardage, and he shrugged as in "I have no idea." I estimated five hundred yards and wondered how in the world Angel spotted him without optical aide as the cactus mostly hid him. He appeared to be looking a different direction, so I asked Dee about closing the distance. We worked for about twenty minutes in and around the rocks, and it looked like we had cut the distance in half. I set up for the shot, but I could not get comfortable.

I had so many thoughts going through my mind at this point that I had to take a moment to say a short prayer and ask God to settle my nerves. I found a rock to use as a rest for the .300 Weatherby and put my backpack on top of it. I decided I would take the shot with the ram bedded because if he saw us and got up, I would have only a moment for a running shot before he disappeared into the rocks. One shot and the ram stood and quickly tumbled to a stop. I had my ram.

It took us about thirty minutes to get to where he fell, and I was almost afraid to get there. For those hunters out there, I am sure at some point in your hunting, you have experienced "ground shrinkage." You know, the animal looks great in your scope or binoculars, and you make the shot, walk up, and are just a little disappointed by the size of the horns or body. Ground shrinkage was not a part of this hunt as the ram was even better than I thought. I took time again for a short prayer of thanks. This had been an incredible experience. How could it have been any better?

The picture taking was some of the most enjoyable I had had to date. We could position the ram anywhere because of all the extra hands. Normally, it was just me and the guide trying to maneuver the animal for great pictures. I was unable to get Angel in a picture with the ram as he was superstitious about pictures. It is interesting to note that the following morning, I did get a picture with Angel as he had spent the entire night drinking vodka. I guess that was his liquid courage.

Let me recap. We chased the ram down the side of the mountain. Next, we found his track at the base of the mountain. Angel and the guys tracked him seven miles across the desert to another mountain. We drove around the entire base of this new mountain and figured the ram was still there. We then went around to the place where the track started and followed Angel as he climbed after the ram. It was hard to see the tracks, but they were there, and one of them was crooked. Angel spotted Old Crooked-Foot hiding among the cactus at five hundred yards with his bare eyes, and I went up and got him with one shot.

Dee and I with Old Crooked Foot

I now had my fourth ram, completing my grand slam of sheep. I sent the remainder of my information for this sheep to the Grand Slam Club. I had previously documented my three other rams. They were satisfied that I had taken all four rams legally, and I was assigned number 705 in the club. This meant that I am the 705th hunter to have legally taken and registered the four mountain sheep from North America since the club began documenting all the way back to 1950. The four species are the Dall, the Stone, the Rocky Mountain bighorn, and the desert bighorn. This award is so special to me because of the small group of hunters who had achieved it. I now had a total of twelve species of the North American 29. What an incredible story!

CHAPTER 10

Muy Grande

Most big game hunters have a favorite species. Although sheep hunting is my favorite type of hunt because I love the steep mountains and the seemingly never-ending blown stalks, they are not my first choice when I analyze my favorite species. The Alaskan brown bear holds my fascination just for the fact that it is the biggest bear in the world. The white-tailed deer and elk are probably the favorites for the majority of North American hunters. A very close third would be the mule deer. My favorite species of North American big game animal, without a doubt, is the mule deer. I have hunted them more than any other species of deer. I enjoy the habitat they occupy. They may be the most elusive species in North America from which to bag a trophy-size animal. The big ones have certainly eluded me for over eighteen years. I have taken some well-above-average bucks, but I have yet to take one that has all the points of his horns in the right place.

The Safari Club International recognizes two species of mule deer. They are the Rocky Mountain mule deer and the desert mule deer. I won't go into the boundaries here that separate the species as there are other books that will do a great job of that. In this chapter, I would like to relate some of my desert mule deer stories. The only place I have hunted desert "muleys" is in the Sonoran Desert in Sonora, Mexico. These hunts have been a wonderful experience.

I have been on three different hunts with two different outfitters. Both outfitters and their guides hunted the same way. The general practice is to be somewhere in the desert before light so you can look around and then spend the day roaming around the desert, looking for tracks or the animals. The guides are all excellent trackers and can tell if the deer is big or not by the size of the track. You will recall the tremendous ability Angel possessed when I took my desert bighorn in 1997.

In January 1993, I hunted with the Campillo Brothers for desert mule deer. Brother Dave and good friend Dan Wilson were also here hunting. Bobbi Campillo ran the camp and provided a first-class hunt. I was teamed up with Philip, an older guide, who had loads of experience. It was day number 2 of a planned five-day hunt. Yesterday, we covered about twelve miles as we crisscrossed the desert, looking for a fresh track. During the afternoon, we followed a single track for about a mile. Philip gave up on it as I think it was too old. The muleys tend to live in the flat areas of the desert. Their cousins, the Coues deer, are generally in the steeper mountainous areas. We caught glimpses of a few more deer butts as they were escaping our intrusion into their homes. Today we were in a new area, but nothing to be seen. Philip spoke no English, so I had not a clue about the game plan. I kept my rifle on ready and remained alert as we walked around in the desert.

Around 10:00 a.m., Philip started yelling at me, "Senor, shoot, shoot! Senor, *muy grande*." I was obviously not looking where he was as I couldn't even see a deer. He was insistent and continued yelling. In between yells, he was pointing at the base of a small hill, and I finally caught a glimpse of the buck. The buck was bouncing as muleys do when they are running at top speed. Phillip yelled some more "*Muy grande!* Shoot, Senor!" I saw horns but had no idea the size of this deer. All I could think was YOU'VE GOT TO BE KIDDING. I had never shot at a running animal at this yardage. I quickly estimated the shot would be about 350 yards. I raised the gun and fired a shot at the very fast running target. The shot was good, and the deer collapsed.

Philip was still excited and yelled something in Spanish that I didn't understand. I found out later at the camp as Bobbi interpreted that he was telling me what a fantastic shot I made. We gave the buck fifteen minutes before we head to it. It was a 345-yard running shot. Although the shot turned out great, I was disappointed in myself for shooting as I would feel terrible if I had wounded the buck. "Muy Grande" was very nice, and I was thankful to God. He was certainly not as good as I was hoping for. It was not that the buck was small; actually, it was bigger than average. It just lacked the points in the right places. He was a five by four and lacked a fork on the back of his left side.

Check out the "walter wayback" hat on that hunter

I learned on this hunt that the shooting at these deer is usually very fast and there is no time for judging trophy size. The guides have very keen eyes, and if you could spot the deer at the same time they do, you might have a chance to judge the size. Usually, by the time the hunter can get the scope on them, they are running or have disappeared into the desert foliage.

When we returned to the camp, Bobbi was very pleased with the buck. We spent the better part of three hours taking pictures. You would have thought we were in Hollywood. They had special lights and aluminum fixtures to focus the light. We were constantly dragging the buck up and down a small hill and repositioning for different photos. I even had to wear a special hat. All I could say was "YOU'VE GOT TO BE KIDDING."

My brother Herb had somewhat the same experience I had. Later in the day on day number 3, the guide was yelling for him to shoot. It took Herb a long time to find the buck his guide was excited about, but eventually, he found him and fired a shot. The buck immediately disappeared, and Herb thought he had made a great shot. The guide looked disgusted and headed toward the area the truck had been parked. Herb assumed they were going to take the truck and pick up the buck. Instead, they drove the opposite way, picked up Dan and his guide who were hunting close by, and headed back to the camp. Perplexed, my brother asked why they hadn't gone to the buck. His guide explained in Spanish, and Bobbi interpreted, that the guide was sure my brother had missed.

I know Herb was thinking, YOU'VE GOT TO BE KIDDING. I talked with him later as we sipped on Tecates around the campfire, and he said it was almost unbelievable that they hadn't at least checked the area for blood or even the buck. Herb shoots a .300 Weatherby also, and the deer could easily have dropped straight down after the shot, giving his guide the impression of a clean miss. He was terribly disappointed and would have to wait for another hunt to collect his trophy desert muley.

My friend Dan connected on a very beautiful heavy-horned buck on the last day of the hunt. The buck scored 184 and something, making his hunt very successful. It was funny to be around Dan on this hunt. He and Bobbi's brother, Ramone, would get into the Margaretas every night. These are not the typical drinks that we have in the United States. They had probably twice the alcohol content, and Dan was enjoying them. The problem was the excessive thirst he encountered every day while walking around the desert. Herb and I thought the weather, which was about 75 degrees during the day, was perfect. We just had to laugh as Dan complained about it being too hot.

My next hunt for desert mule deer took place in 1998. This was for free, but I shouldn't use the word "free" here as it really cost me $60,000. It is the hunt I received from Ernesto Zaragoza when I did the desert bighorn hunt with him in 1997. That sheep hunt I had with Ernesto had been such a huge success that I invited two of my brothers, Herb and Steve, and a good friend, Reese, along to share this mule deer hunt. Once again, mine was the "freebie," so I was pretty relaxed, and I told Ernesto to cater to my family and friend.

Let's get real, it's just an average deer

Ernesto had two ranches we would be hunting. Both places had very nice accommodations. They were quite a distance apart, and we lost a great deal of hunting time when we had to move between the ranches. If I could slight Ernesto any, it would be for this moving. It took us a half day to get from one to the other. In the end, Steve and Reese collected little deer. They found the scenario of shooting before judging, produced at least for them, less-than-trophy animals. Herb and I never had a chance at a good buck. We would have to wait for another time. I was very fortunate in that I found a buck that had been killed by a mountain lion. I brought those horns home and did a beautiful mount. There was one very nice buck taken by a nice older gentleman as they drove out of camp one morning. The driver was only five hundred yards down the road when they spotted the dear right along the road.

This story is very typical of desert mule deer hunting. The trophies are there; it's a matter of luck to be in the right spot. Contrast this with some hunts, such as mountain sheep, where the hunter can sway the luck in his favor by the physical ability to go after a trophy once it's been spotted.

I returned in 1999 to hunt again with Ernesto. I made this trip alone as I felt so bad about the last trip when no one scored on any trophies. This time my guide spoke a little English, so it was quite enjoyable. We were hunting one of the ranches we had done before. There was no travel time between ranches this time as we stayed right at the Americano ranch. The weather again was perfect. This was the fifth time I had hunted in Sonora, and I have never had any bad weather.

My guide and I hunted hard for four days. We tracked a few bucks, but they were really on the move as the rut was in full force. My guide told me they were almost impossible to catch up with during the rut. I thought, *I was going to say that, but you beat me to it.* You know my philosophy about guides; they are always right.

Today we were going to do mostly road hunting. He said there were a few roads in the area that allowed us a vantage point above the desert floor, and maybe we could catch something moving. With this being my third attempt at these deer, I was open to almost any strategic plan. It was kind of fun sitting in the jump seat in the back of the jeep, but I was having withdrawals because I was not getting scratched by thorns. You've heard me say all the desert plants have thorns, and I'm usually in them.

We were approaching the noon hour, and my guide said we would go up the small mountain in front of us and sit and glass while we eat lunch. On this hunt, we had hot lunches as my guide had brought along a cookstove, which we used to make our bologna sandwiches into gourmet meals by warming and adding real goat cheese and jalapeños. Just as we started devouring our five-star lunch, they appeared on the ridge. A group of eight does, about 275 yards away. Surely, with the rut occurring, there would be a buck with them. They were moving a fair speed but not running all out. Aware of us but moving sideways to our spot, they were not spooked. We waited.

How easily the desert plants hide large animals. The buck was moving, but we never got a chance to see him completely. As he approached another organ pipe cactus, my guide was yelling the standard desert muley lingo: *"Muy grande!* Shoot, Senor!"* I had been watching right along with him, and I couldn't tell if it was *muy grande* or *pequenito*. I couldn't take the chance that he was a good trophy and I missed the opportunity, so I put the scope on him and shoot. I took the deer with one shot. My guide was high-fiving me, but I said, "Let's give it fifteen minutes and then go and see." I was sure the .300 Weatherby had done its job again, but the desert was lush, and we couldn't see the deer.

After the walk out to the ridge, we found the buck, and he was very good. Now I could high five my guide. The rack was tall and heavy. A perfect five by five, you say? Not so as it was another buck missing a few parts. Of course, I had to say, "YOU'VE GOT TO BE KIDDING." It would appear my destiny did not include a nice, perfect desert mule deer. I cared, but he was well above average and better than my previous desert bucks, so I was thrilled. The idea that he came by while we were having lunch was a great feeling, and I was again thankful to God for my success. This brought my count of North American species to thirteen.

Another desert mule deer from Sonora

CHAPTER 11

Couple's Retreat

The hunting trip in this chapter is without a doubt my favorite. The thing that made this trip so special was that Becky was able to share it with me. We had wanted to do a hunting trip together since 1992 when Becky gave up her chance to go with me to Gillette, Wyoming. Now it is August of 2000, and we are going to British Columbia. We will be there for two weeks as I try for three more species of big game. I will hunt Western Canadian moose, and then mountain goat, and finally, mountain caribou. We are going to be the guests of Art and Crystal Thompson, who operate Gundahoo River Outfitters at Muncho Lake, British Columbia. Once again, Gregg Severinson, the manager at Cabela's Outdoor Adventures, has done his homework and then recommended Art and Crystal as the best place to go for the three species I wanted to hunt.

A little update on my North American "29" is in order. Last year, I got a desert mule deer, thus bringing my total to thirteen different species. If you recall last year, 1999, I returned to hunt desert mule deer with Ernesto Zaragoza. The hunt in 1998 with Ernesto was a freebie as part of booking my desert bighorn sheep hunt, which I had hunted in February 1997. I had mortgaged the farm, and kids, and all my future earnings to pay the $60,000 it took for that sheep hunt. Because the cost was so high, I think Ernesto Zaragoza felt guilty and gave me a free desert mule deer hunt. It took some doing to earn back the $60,000, but we ended up having pretty good crops for the years 1998 and 1999. We also were very busy with our custom harvest operation. Consequently, my banker was happy that I had made some progress in debt reduction. This scenario will be short-lived, though, as you will see later in the book.

The overall tone for this book is some humor and a very positive attitude in life. Without changing that concept, I do have to mention something very sad that happened at the end of 1999. Actually, it happened on my forty-sixth birthday on December 28, 1999. My very good friend Jim Freeburg had fought a two-year battle with cancer and lost the fight that day. He was only forty years old, and Becky and I lost a wonderful friend and neighbor. He was always a planner, and I'm amazed how he made sure I would never forget the date of his passing. How incredible that God planned for him to leave this Earth on my birthday. Jim was a dedicated pheasant and deer hunter. He had ambitions to do more big game hunting, but his illness got in the way of that. We have all heard the remark "Go hunting while you are able." Many times, we think we have to wait until we have all our finances in order before we start with big game hunting trips. I have seen so many people who, at that point in life when they finally have enough money, are physically unable to go hunting. As you've seen in these chapters, I pushed my finances very hard so I could utilize my good health.

I haven't pursued three species of animals on any given hunt since 1992 on my first trip to Alaska. I am sure this hunt will be as successful as that trip was. Becky and I made a few extra trips to Cabela's before we left for this hunt as I wanted to make sure she had the proper equipment. I think she really enjoyed the

Becky, happy to be going hunting

challenge of finding the proper boots, rain gear, backpack, and even camouflaged lingerie. It was funny the excitement we could generate among the two of us as we talked about how the experience would be. We were looking forward to quality time spent together without any phones, TVs, or problems with the farm or hired help. We were hoping that the spike camps could also accommodate Becky so she could experience the actual hunt as an observer.

On Friday, August 25, at 5:00 p.m., we were all packed and seated on the plane in Aberdeen, South Dakota. The trip goes from here to Minneapolis and then the red-eye to Edmonton, Alberta. After a short night in Edmonton, we are to fly to Fort Nelson, British Columbia. Art and Crystal are to meet us at the airport. Unlike the 1992 Alaska trip, there are no restrictions on the weight of our gear. That made it easy to pack, but we brought far too much stuff. We are just getting relaxed and a half hour into the short flight to Minneapolis when the announcement comes over the intercom that there is thunderstorm right over the airport in Minneapolis. We are going to wait it out by flying around, and if it doesn't move quickly through the area, we are going to divert to another airport. I thought I heard them say the alternate would be Chicago. If you are thinking right at this point that this delay to getting on the ground in Minneapolis sounds familiar, you are right. Do you remember in chapter 5 the broken airplane in Watertown, South Dakota, and the charter flight to enable me to get to Edmonton? Well, as we spend in excess of forty-five minutes circling but finally land, we are left with ten minutes to get to our Edmonton flight. As mentioned in an earlier chapter, we fly a small turbo propjet from Aberdeen, and you land at the far end of the airport. Well, there is no way to make our flight, but we run and try anyway. At the gate, the ticket agent informs us that the plane is pushing back and we cannot get aboard. Now this time it is Becky who says the famous words "YOU'VE GOT TO BE KIDDING."

The gate agent says we should head down to the ticket counter and see what they can do for us. We ask about our bags, and she says they should be able to find them for us at the ticket counter. When we get there, we ask again about our bags. They track our baggage claim tickets, and you'll never guess where our bags are to be found. They are on the airplane we just missed. I said, "Whatever," thinking she was teasing us, but when we realize she is serious, I can't hold back from saying it. "YOU'VE GOT TO BE KIDDING." How in the world could they get our bags off the Aberdeen plane and onto the Edmonton flight faster than the ten minutes it took for us to get from our Aberdeen flight to the gate for the Edmonton plane? It really is more funny than unbelievable, especially when you normally wait thirty minutes at baggage claim to get bags.

After about a half hour of organizing and checking flights with the ticket agent, our only solution is the following: Because there are no more flights from Minneapolis to Edmonton for the evening, we fly to Seattle. From there, we rent a car about two thirty in the morning and drive the rest of the night to Vancouver, British Columbia. We get there about six thirty and just barely catch the flight to Fort Nelson, British Columbia.

We are met at the airport and visit with our new family, the Thompsons. They will be our life for the next two weeks. As we wait at baggage claim for our luggage, they make us feel so comfortable and welcome. However, guess what. No bags arrive. They take the time to search our original claim tickets and find our bags in Las Vegas. How I kept from letting my Irish heritage kick into gear, I don't know, but we are disappointed to say the least. I really am proud of myself at times because most of the time, I just blow up and start swearing and yelling. They assure us that they will deliver our bags to us as soon as they arrive in Fort Nelson. Now we are headed about 150 miles west and some north from Fort Nelson to Muncho Lake, British Columbia, and I smirk as I think they have no idea that they will have to deliver them to Art's hunting camp. I'm wondering how often this happens in the world of hunting. The biggest worry for me is my rifle not getting here, and I can't meet my goal of taking all the species with the same rifle.

The drive to Muncho Lake along the Alaskan Highway is very picturesque. We pass a fold mountain, which is a very unique mountain that looks like a sandwich with lots of layers of meats standing on end instead of lying flat. Art keeps a horse barn in the small town of Muncho Lake, and we stop to get a trailer and some horses and head to the camp. We can already see the attention to detail that Art and Crystal are famous for, and their equipment and the base camp are impeccably maintained. After being settled in, we are introduced to Crystal's fine cooking. I don't know how but all the outfitters I've hunted with have gone over and above when it comes to the quality of the meals they put out for the hunters. If you think you are going to lose any weight going on these hunts, just forget it. You will be lucky if you don't gain 10 pounds. Becky had a good time comparing cooking recipes and foods with Crystal and her staff.

After we eat, Art lays out the tentative plan for the two weeks of hunting. We will lose one day, which is tomorrow, as we have to wait for the baggage. Art has cabins spread out in the 7,500 square miles that make up his hunting territory. This is a huge area. It is always refreshing to the hunter when the outfitter has so much area to hunt. We are so excited to be here, and the more Art and Crystal talk, we can see this is a first-class operation. I hope that tomorrow Art is going to fly me to the camp on some of the headwaters of the

Gundahoo River Base Camp

Gundahoo River. Then he will return to bring Becky out to the camp on the next trip. The camp is called Game Creek, and from there, we will hunt Canadian moose. It may be possible to run into a few mountain caribou at the same time but no mountain goats as we are not in steep enough mountains to support goat populations.

Actually, the season for goats and grizzly bear doesn't open until August 31. Tomorrow is the twenty-seventh, and if we can fly to the camp, we won't hunt until the twenty-eighth. That will give me three days for moose before the other seasons open. Oh, by the way, this time I have a grizzly bear tag, and I'm hoping I will run across a bear sometime during this hunt. If you recall back to the 1992 Alaska hunt, I had three bears following us the day we were moving the meat from my Alaskan moose, but I didn't have a tag. If successful with the moose, we are then going to move to the cabin at Fish Lake, which is a much better caribou country. Then after that, we will move to a cabin at much higher elevation to hunt the goat. If this sounds like a lot of flying and moving, it is. The good outfitters have such huge territories, such as Art's, that flying is a huge part of their business. Now as I mentioned in an earlier chapter, Becky's favorite thing is not flying. I can see the look in her beautiful big green eyes as Art continues to talk about all the trips. She has never flown in any kind of bush plane, so I am also a little worried. She has brought along some extra Dramamine, which will help her with the bumps that are encountered when flying in the mountains. We end the day with a two-hour hike around the camp.

The morning dawned with a light rain and heavy fog. They called from the Fort Nelson airport and said our bags were in, but they wouldn't be able to bring them to us as they said they would never find the camp. Oh boy! Crystal said she would make the three-hundred-mile round trip and get them for us. While she is gone, the weather gets worse, so even if we had our bags, we couldn't have flown out to Game Creek today. We enjoyed a day of cribbage, book reading, and, of course, the wonderful food.

The next morning was about the same weather, and I welcomed Becky to North Country, where there can be long periods of waiting to fly. About noon, the fog went away, and Art and I load the plane and head to Game Creek. This flight, like many I have been on, is incredible. The scenery in many parts of this beautiful world will live in my memory forever. The valleys are so green, the mountains are so steep, and there is wildlife everywhere. I can't imagine what Becky will be thinking as she makes her first trip to a spike camp. I hope she will be as impressed as I always am.

Art's impecably maintained air taxi

We land at the cabin, and I meet my guide, Aaron Friedlund. I have only seen him for two seconds, and I am already pissed. You would think just one time I could get a guide who was short and squatty like I am. You know that would be my only chance to keep up with him when we are climbing and hiking. Anyway, kidding aside, Aaron is six feet four inches, and his smile puts me at ease right away. He and I will spend the next fourteen days hunting, so I'm glad he strikes me as being easygoing. As Aaron and I unpack my gear, Art and Jessica (Aaron's wife who has been staying in the spike camp) head back to the base camp to get Becky. Aaron lays out the plan and direction we will go to hunt moose tomorrow. It gets late, and Becky has not arrived. Aaron says the fog probably returned, and

Art's plane would end up grounded. I don't like to hear that, but I can't change the situation.

Cabin at Game creek with Art (left) and Aaron and Jessica

The next morning, we are up early, eat breakfast, and then Aaron goes to find the horses. He comes back, and I then meet my ride for the next two weeks. His name is Hammer, and he is a mule. Now I've never ridden a mule, so I don't judge on the spot. I will give him a chance to show me how good he is. Right away, I have a problem. I am too short, or he is too tall, and I can't get up on him without some sort of stepping-stone. A ladder would be the real deal. We have only been away from the camp a few hours, and I already have a new name for Hammer. We have been riding in some pretty heavy timber, and every time he goes by tree, he sidesteps and jams my leg and rifle into the tree trunk. Now I finally yell at him, "YOU'VE GOT TO BE KIDDING!" I guess he doesn't understand English as he continues to do it. Therefore, I tell Aaron his name has just been changed to Jammer. I thought he was going to fall off his horse laughing.

Hammer alias "Jammer"

As we ride among the trees, we spot a few moose but only see them for a few minutes. Aaron says not to worry as these are only cows. The big boys hang out at the top of the mountains this time of year. After about another hour, we start up the mountains. This is refreshing as Jammer has nothing to jam me against, but I'm sure he is scheming something else. He isn't all bad as he produces a very smooth ride compared with a horse. He is like a Cadillac, and a horse is just a Chevrolet. We actually ride most of the way to the top. We have a little lunch, and Aaron says we'll use the high vantage point we have to glass the surrounding peaks and valleys for moose or caribou. He has a very good spotting scope, and we find many animals to look over. About 3:00 p.m., he spots three moose at the top of a very tall mountain to our north. The one bull looks very big, even though we estimate him to be four miles away. Aaron says we will go and get him . . . tomorrow. Now I'm thinking that in most hunting I've done, the quarry will be long gone if you wait until tomorrow. What I don't realize is the four miles across the top represents almost a day of travel to get down, go across, and then go all the way up.

115

That night, sleep was hard to get as I am so disappointed that Becky

Our camping "buddy"

hasn't made it here yet. Evidently, the weather at the base camp, which is sixty miles away, must still be fogged in.

Aaron and I have started to establish a friendship as we are giving each other some pretty good-natured insults. He has a name for me, which is "Potlicker." Now I should be hurt as I know in Canada, the name means you lick toilets. I really don't want to get upset as I do need Aaron to be working for

me for another thirteen days. I am mulling around in my mind a few names for him, but I haven't used any yet. OK, I did sarcastically call him "Master Guide" a few times. I think this got him because I had a way of saying

The things you see when the season isn't open

it that made him sound like a rookie guide. Hey, you have to stand up for yourself!

The next morning, as we get ready to head up the mountain where the bull moose are, what happens next is the ultimate "YOU'VE GOT TO BE KIDDING" for this hunt. We are just getting on our rides when Aaron's horse starts acting crazy. We look at each other as to say we don't know what's up. Then we see him. He is heading right for us. We both think he will stop, but he continues toward the cabin and actually at one point scoots under the fence in front of the cabin, stands there, and looks at us. Now as I said earlier in this chapter, I have a grizzly bear tag, and I now have a very nice seven-and-a-half-footer grizzly less than thirty yards from me. He is gorgeous with lots of silver tip hair and very good hide with no rub marks. Now you are thinking how lucky can I be? He just walked right up to the hunter. However, as usual, "Houston, we have a problem." The bear is here today at the cabin, but my hunting tag for grizzly bear is not any good until tomorrow. Now who would have guessed that scenario? Sure, I could have taken him, no one would know, but rules and seasons have to be honored. This is why North American hunters are respected worldwide, because we make every effort to support conservation efforts and laws that ensure we have quality animals to hunt.

Top of the mountain Canada moose

We got over the sadness of watching him amber away and got back in the saddle and head out for moose. Aaron thought we might see him again, especially if we had some moose meat in the camp. I was hoping I would get my moose today to have an attractant in the camp. The first part of the ride takes us the heavy timber in the valley, and Jammer continues to live up to his name. We then start up the mountain where we saw the three bull moose yesterday. It becomes very steep about half the way up, so we tether the horse and Jammer to a small shrub, and we go on foot. We are going up very fast, and I think again about the excellent condition of the guides I've hunted with over the years. Aaron is very good, and he asks me often how the old "potlicker" is doing. Even if I weren't doing fine, I would still tell him great. The light rain has turned to a bit of a mixture of rain and sleet as we near the top, but the visibility is still fair.

I'm not sure how the "master guide" has done it, but as we get to the top, sure enough, three bull moose are standing about 350 yards from us. We have the wind in our favor, so we use the ground cover to shorten the distance. We are about 200 yards away, and they decide they will lie down. As they do lie, we cannot see them. We close the distance a little, but the wind is now swirling, and Aaron says we had better stop as to not let them wind us. The waiting game begins, and

the snow is a bit heavier. I tell myself to make sure to pull the scope cover off before I take aim when they stand. The idea that I would forget makes me nervous, so I take the cover off now. The snow accumulates on the scope, and I keep wiping the lenses clean, but at least I'm ready. Then it happens. The big boys stand, and I find the best one, which looks very good. I think I miss with the first shot as my scope is hard to see in because I didn't get all the

Well above average at 54"

118

snow out, so I clean and fire again. This time the Weatherby has done its job. We wait about fifteen minutes, and I say my prayers of thanks. We then walk up and find him in the same little hollow he had been lying in while we waited earlier. We got right to work with pictures and trophy care.

After the pictures, I am looking at the size of this animal and reflect to the day I got my Alaskan moose. We spent all day getting that 1,600 pounds handled, and this moose doesn't look much smaller. Aaron says that we probably can go back down to Jammer and his horses and slowly lead them up this steep mountain and load the moose right where he lies. You know I'm all for that idea. I tell Aaron after such a great plan, "That's the reason he gets paid the big bucks." He just shakes his head and smirks. We get the mule and the two horses Aaron has brought and get the moose taken care and loaded. Now I learn something I did not know until now. Some horses will not carry a load of meat from a dead animal. They simply go berserk. We loaded everything and then switch all the meat to the horse Aaron has ridden, and he will have to ride the packhorse back to the camp.

We get back to the camp after dark and hang the moose meat on the meat pole to keep it away from the bears. Our friendly grizzly was not seen, which is probably good as we don't want to worry that he might ruin or take the horns or the hide.

As great as this day is, I am sad as Becky is still not in the camp. I can only hope and pray that in the morning, Art might show up with my bride. At least at the base camp, she has people to keep her company. Tomorrow we are going to pack up and ride our packhorse train over the mountains to the next hunting cabin at Fish Lake. We would hunt caribou along the way. I am so grateful to have taken such a tremendous moose, especially so early in the hunt. That would allow more time for the other two animals.

The morning came, and we finished work on the moose, including getting the hide all done. Still, no sign of Becky, and now we are leaving this camp. It will be just my luck, or should I say that guy "Murphy" will act and Art will fly her here and we will be gone.

The trip over to the Fish Lake cabin produces a look at a few herds of caribou, but there are no good bulls with them. Our plan is to hunt from this cabin for a few days and then head over the snowy peaks to the goat camp. We aren't able to spot any bears either. After the first night, Aaron and I talked about the runway here at this camp. It seems that for Art to land, the wind has to be minimal, thus adding to the problem of seeing Becky in the spike camp. It is getting a little frustrating as we've been apart about six days now. Our dream trip of relaxing and being together certainly hasn't gone as planned. I did tell Becky before we left home that the weather in the northern wilderness areas plays such a huge role in planning. Many days are lost because of poor visibility, rain, or snow.

Day 2 at this camp produces hardly a glimpse at any animals. We see a few scattered caribou, but again, nothing of the size we are looking for. As we return in the evening, I am getting a feeling that Becky will be at the camp, but she is not. Now again I have to say those famous words to Aaron, "YOU'VE GOT TO BE KIDDING." We plan to try one more day here for caribou before we will leave tomorrow morning to try for my mountain caribou. Aaron thinks the caribou are still up high, and we will have better luck on the other side of the mountains. The day, like yesterday, is quiet, and as evening nears, we are in the camp when we hear Art's airplane. My heart leaps as I know Becky is here. Sure enough, the weather conditions allowed for flying, and Becky is finally here at the spike camp. We enjoyed our one night together before I left for the mountain goat camp. I hope Art would be able to come and fly her over to the goat hunting camp, which is about twenty miles away.

Fish Lake cabin, Becky and Jessica's home for six days

So Aaron and I are packed and loaded. We are heading up and over the pass to get to the goats. He says the snow will be deep as we cross, and the trail is very steep. We will have to lead our horses and mule a great distance. We ride, and the new scenery is beautiful. It seems like around every corner is another valley that looks nothing like the last one but equally as beautiful. I can see as we get closer to the snowy peaks that there will be some very steep terrain.

We are now heading up the steep part of the trail. It has become very icy and snowy. Aaron says we can't ride anymore. It seems to be straight up, and Aaron notices I am not keeping up and offers a great idea. He says to go around to the butt end of Jammer and grab his tail. Now I think, *Yeah right, I am just going to grab his tail, and he is going to be OK with that.* The idea here is to actually use Jammer to pull me up the mountain. Now you guys know Jammer, and he will do something foolish and make me look bad. However, guess what, the master guide is right again, and Jammer pulls me up the mountain. By now, we are traveling in knee-deep snow, and I'm so grateful for the help. As we approach the summit, Jammer is just trucking along, and I see the top. There is a sheer cliff right in front of us, and Jammer is still going. I think he is going over the edge with

121

me in tow. I yell at Aaron, "What the hell should I do?" He calmly replies, "Let go of his tail, and he will stop." Now honestly, you would think I could have come up with that idea. I felt so stupid.

We start down the other side, get to camp with enough daylight to get unpacked, and organize to hunt in the morning. I am praying that Becky and Jessica will be safe back at Fish Lake and that the weather will cooperate as to allow her to join me here. I never thought we would see so little of each other and be on the same vacation. Oh, by the way, the girls were a little mad when we left this morning because of one more situation. They have a shotgun at the cabin to take with them when they go to the creek to retrieve water. This will be their protection in case of bear trouble. The issue is there are only three shells for the gun. They are actually quite pissed about this, and I guess I can't blame them. I pray to God that they remain safe.

Beautiful scenery on trip to mountain goat country

The morning sun is very welcome today as yesterday, it was very gloomy and a light rain. Today it is warm, and it seems like a lucky day. We'll see. We ride about two hours and find a mountainside where Aaron has spotted a very large goat in the past. He has eluded more than one hunter, but we are going to see if we can find him.

The mountain is unbelievably steep, and even if we spot him, I don't know how we could ever get to him. I am not overly comfortable with heights, and this mountain looks as if we should have climbing gear. We glass the mountain for over four hours, and Aaron spots him. We set the scope up, and he is huge. We think pushing the ten-inch mark, but he is quite a ways from us. Our plan now is to see if he will come down even a little. We wait until almost dark and decide to come back tomorrow and find him again. Back at the camp, it is quiet as Art has not been here. I pray again and hope that Art has gotten Becky from Fish Lake and returned with her to the base camp.

After a quiet night, the morning is again beautiful and sunny. We have left the camp earlier today in hopes we might the catch the "billy" a little lower today. We again find him and watch all day. He goes nowhere, and at almost dark, we return to the camp. Once again, the camp is deserted. Aaron says that in the morning, we will look again for the goat, but if he is still in the same place, which is where we can't see him, we are going to look for another goat. He assures me there is more than one goat in these mountains and would have to agree. I have only five days left to find a goat, a bear, and a caribou.

The next morning, we find the goat again, and guess what, he is still in the same place. I would like to try for this huge "billy," but I really am not comfortable with heights anymore. I don't want Aaron to work very hard to get us started up the mountain and then I couldn't make it all the way. So we begin the search for a different goat. Lady luck is on our side as only an hour later on a mountain directly across the one we had watched for three days, we spot another "billy." He is a bit smaller but certainly a fine trophy. We start up after him. The mountain I'm climbing may be as steep as the one I had just passed on. The climb takes us through a large area of supersized boulders, and these become a challenge as we struggle to get over and through them. It is taking us a great deal of time to get where we need to be, but our goat is still in about the same place. We started after him about eight thirty, and now it is two o'clock, and we finally have gotten above him. We close the distance to about 125 yards, and I take one shot and have my mountain goat. Now he begins to

On the way up Blender Mountain

roll, and I think back to my Rocky Mountain bighorn and hope the goat will stop as the sheep did. Aaron on the way up this mountain had explained to me that it is called blender mountain. I ask why, and he says, "Well, the hunters that have taken goats here before have watched as their trophies have rolled from the top to the bottom, and consequently, they look as if they have been through a blender." Now as my goat is rolling, I think, *Blender mountain,* YOU'VE GOT TO BE KIDDING. I am expecting the worst when suddenly, he stops. Then I say, "Thank you, God." It takes us a good forty-five minutes to get to him, and he is a great goat. I am so happy to have him. Picture taking and trophy care are almost impossible at this angle, but we manage.

The pack trip down was a great challenge because of the steepness, but it was downhill. We made good time and got back to the camp before dark.

Once again, it is Aaron and I at the camp. I still have not seen Becky here, and now there are only four days of the hunt left. I say some more prayers that everything is OK. Our plan for the morning is to head a different direction to search for the caribou. Aaron says we won't have any trouble getting a good bull with four days to hunt. It will require some physical exertion, but I'm OK with that.

Aaron and the "billy", Who's got the best beard?

The next two days we see a great number of caribou, but they are always miles away, and we haven't had a real chance to get one. Then about 3:00 p.m., we find a good bull at the bottom of a very deep canyon. He is thrashing a small tree as he attempts to clean his horns of velvet. We make the decision to go down and get him. We are about an hour into the stalk when he decides he is going up the other side of the canyon. Now because of the size of this canyon, the only chance we have is to go back the way we just had hiked, get the horses and Jammer, and try to get around the other side of the canyon before he gets to the top. This is where it pays to be in shape as Aaron is practically running up the side of the canyon. I'm getting behind, but I'm not quitting because this is a nice bull and the best one we've seen in twelve days of hunting.

125

We get to our rides, and the trip around the end of the canyon where we actually can cross with the horses takes us a long time.

Two old goats!

When we finally get where we think our bull should be, there he is. A quick dismount, OK, a slow dismount because it's Jammer, and he hasn't gotten any shorter, and I have my rifle on him. I don't even look at the size of the horns, and with one shot, he is down. Now Aaron takes off like a "wild man" and heads to the bull. I have no idea what he is doing, and he really is fast. He gets to the bull, grabs him by the horns, and yells at me, "I got him!" I guess I was thinking that I was the one who got him. As I got over to him, I understood the emergency. Right behind Aaron was a sheer cliff, and if he hadn't stopped the caribou from a short roll, I would have lost him. Now I'm thinking, *What's with all the rolling animals?* We have saved two on this hunt alone.

The reason they are called mountain caribou

We get some really good pictures and make fast work of getting the bull taken care of. I have never seen a more luxurious coat of hair on any other caribou. His is so thick. We hadn't realized how far we had gotten ourselves from the camp, so it was after dark when we got back. Once again, no Becky. All I can say is I'm going to have one upset Norwegian wife when and if we ever get together again. It seems almost unbelievable how this has all gone down. I have taken three wonderful animals, and Becky has not seen any of it. I sure wish it could have worked differently. Aaron says in the morning the best thing we can do is leave early on the horses and Jammer and actually go all the way to Muncho Lake. I guess I won't question him as I have no idea where and how far it would be to Muncho Lake.

My great mountain caribou

That night, I thanked God for an incredible experience and the fine trophies. I also asked him to let me live when I eventually ran into Becky again. The next morning, just as Aaron had planned, we loaded and left early. Sometime about one o'clock, I got my first real views of Muncho Lake. We were so high above that it provided with an absolutely breathtaking view. Aaron informed then that we would have to lead the horses down the mountain and it would take us about four hours to get down. I thought that was too long, but I soon found out.

As Aaron said it would be four hours, what he should have said was it would take normal people six hours, but he was in a huge rush. It was on this descent where I got mad at him. This was my only time I was frustrated with Aaron, but I was having a hell of a time going as fast as we were. I was constantly tripping and falling, and because we were leading the horses, Jammer tried to run me over numerous times. It was really very dangerous, and I couldn't get Aaron slowed down. I suddenly realized he had only seen his wife one night in the last thirteen days, so he was as lonesome as I was. As we approached the bottom, I was beat from head to toe. My face was scratched and bleeding; I had a sprained ankle and sore back and ribs. However, you know I didn't care as we had a short ride to Art's horse barn. There, we had a phone and called the base camp to tell Crystal we were down. She relayed that Becky and Jessica had just gotten back from Fish Lake about an hour ago. Crystal said Becky was not in a good mood. Now as I analyze, Becky stayed at the base camp almost a week and then at Fish lake for five or six days without me. It was no wonder she was mad.

High above Muncho Lake

As we drove up to the base camp, I thought I could see steam coming out through the roof. Becky had to be causing the steam. I was afraid to get too close, but as we got right to the house, Becky came out and was just as thrilled to see me as I was thrilled to see her. It felt good to hug and kiss her. She wasn't happy with the situation, but she is a wonderful, forgiving person and realized the weather trouble that can go hand in hand on these hunts. We did get to be together that night and the next before we had to leave for South Dakota.

Becky had gained a new friend in Jessica. She was very much like our daughter, Nicole. Although they were a bit scared to be out in the wilderness alone, I think Jessica had proved her worth as she

129

took care of the camp and Becky. Then again, maybe Becky took care of Jessica.

Originally, when I went the first day to Game Creek, Art had to fly some of the other hunters from the base camp to their spike camps. Well, when he finished moving them, the weather turned, and he could not fly. When the fog lifted five days later, he got Jessica and Becky to Fish Lake. Then the weather turned again, and he couldn't get them out until the same day we got back. Overall, the Thompsons did all they could do. They provided an exceptional experience for us. Their equipment was first class as was their help. The spike camp cabins were the best I had ever seen. I thought I heard Art say he had thirty of these cabins scattered across his hunting area. What a huge investment!

The cabin used for the goat hunting

We made it home in time to start kidney bean harvest, and then we moved to the corn and soybean harvest. It was a decent year on the farm, but Becky and I were already planning another trip where we could go and not be together again. Ha Ha Ha

CHAPTER 12

Inuit

How far north on planet Earth have you traveled? As you read in chapter 7, my guide Buck and I were hunting white-tailed deer at High Level, Alberta. This is as far north as I had been in Canada. Chapter 2 took me to Deadhorse Alaska, which is on the Arctic Ocean, making that the farthest north I have been in the United States. Now I am about to go on a trip to Nunavut, Canada, to hunt Greenland muskox. I am going to Holman, Victoria Island. Let me try to put in perspective just how far north this is. Most people generally know where Edmonton, Alberta, is located. Edmonton is approximately in the center of Alberta. Next, most people also know that commercial airlines fly around 500-plus miles per hour. To reach Edmonton from Minneapolis takes about three and a half hours. Therefore, factoring in the northwest route and converting to straight north, Edmonton is about 1,100 miles north of South Dakota. To get to Holman from Edmonton, first, we take a commercial flight for two and a half hours to Yellowknife, Northwest Territories, Canada. Thus, you are another 1,200 miles north. Then you take a commercial flight from Yellowknife for another two and a half hours to Holman. Thus, you are again another 1,200 miles north. By the time you reach Holman, you are indeed a long way north.

The thermometer reads -45 degrees Fahrenheit as I board the plane in Yellowknife. We are flying a Canada Air regional jet to Holman. They told me at the check-in that the wind is blowing at Holman and we may not be able to land because of whiteout conditions. I ask what the procedure is if we are unable to land. I'm told we will return to Yellowknife and try tomorrow. It is March

131

2001, and I guess, much like our weather in South Dakota this time of year, there can be a lot of wind. I really am not sure what I should wish for: landing in Holman or returning to Yellowknife. I am very apprehensive about this hunt. Growing up in North Dakota as a child, we experienced winter temperatures down to -45 degrees. The difference is I could tolerate the cold much more easily then. It seems now that anything under 85 is cold.

The plane this morning is a mix of a few hunters and Inuit people. The natives have to make the flight from Holman down to Yellowknife to do their doctoring or dental work. As I chat with them and they tell me about having to travel two and a half hours by plane to see the dentist, I can't imagine how they manage the cost.

Seated next to me is a fellow hunter from Phoenix. It seems very weird that he is a dentist and I would meet him as I am thinking about the Inuit and their dentistry. He is also going muskox hunting. Our plane has one stop in Coppermine, and he is going a different direction from there. We will meet again in a week on the return trip to Yellowknife. We converse about equipment and cold weather gear. At the SCI convention last year, I purchased what I think is the finest cold weather clothing made in the United States. Northern Outfitters from the Salt Lake area produces a complete set of gear especially for the extremes of the Canadian Arctic. For $1,000, I got everything I needed for extreme cold weather, including a -60 degree sleeping bag. My new friend from Arizona was going to use the clothing he got in a local sporting goods store in California. It will be fun to compare notes on equipment when the hunt is over.

It is my lucky day as we land in Holman without incident. The wind is blowing, but I guess the pilot had enough visibility to land safely. The airport terminal is impressive for a village of four hundred people. It rivals what we have locally in Aberdeen, South Dakota, which is over twenty-two thousand people. This won't be the last impressive thing about Holman. Wallace Joss, who will be my guide for the next five or six days, meets me. His English is very good, and I'm thrilled by this. I ask about the temperature as being cold, but he says he has no idea. He says they never worry what the temperature is because they will do whatever they had planned anyway. My baggage is present, and Wally gives me a tour of the "city" as we work our way to the Game and Fish Department to procure my hunting license. I pull out my thermometer, and it's good news, still only -45 degrees.

Wally asks about my hobbies besides hunting, and I mention golf. He drives me a short distance from town, and unbelievably, they have a golf course. This makes Holman the farthest north golf course in North America. He tells me they have a very big tournament every summer as people fly in from surrounding villages, the closest being Coppermine, which is about three hundred miles away. The course is mostly rocks, big and small, and gives new meaning to the term "being in the rough." The tee boxes are square pieces of green indoor/outdoor carpet. The greens are fashioned out of the same carpet. I swear to you I will never complain about the conditions of any golf course after seeing what Wally and his friends call their home course.

Main street in Holman, NWT, Canada

My muskox hunt is with Northwest Adventures from Yellowknife, and I will be there for five days. They use the Inuits from Holman to actually conduct the hunts. In my mind, when looking at these temperatures, if there was to be a time to be lucky and get my trophy on the first day of the hunt, this would be the time. Wally asks me if I just want any muskox or if I am looking for something big. He says most hunters fly into Holman, they then take them just outside of town, and they hunt the local herd. I tell Wally I will go for the next option, that of a very large muskox, and he explains the hunt. We will take two snowmobiles and two wood sleds and travel about two hundred miles east and hunt some herds that aren't usually hunted. I ask about the chances for a very good trophy, and Wally says excellent. After lunch, we embark. I am covered from head to toe, with no exposed skin. At these temperatures, skin can freeze in minutes.

Two snowmobiles were pulling two wood sleds. I ride in one, and the gear we need to survive rides in the other. Wally and his young friend are my snowmobile drivers. Before we left, I had casually asked Wally to give me the rundown of the equipment we are bringing. It's not that I don't trust them, but let's face it, I am concerned to be out five days at -45 degrees and two hundred miles from Holman. So far, my clothing is keeping me warm, but I'm not sure after we get up to speed at 30 mph. Windchill could be -100 degrees. I am amazed thus far as Wally is riding with his face into the wind and has nothing covering it. How can bare skin stand that? He tells me their skin actually freezes but sustains no damage as it is conditioned. Okay, YOU'VE GOT TO BE KIDDING. Just in case you thought you were a tough outdoor type, try to compete with that.

Wally has instructed me to let him know if I get cold. He says they will put up a tent and get me warmed up. We had only gone a mile from Holman when I thought about getting him to stop. I didn't though, and I actually didn't get any colder as the miles passed. I really wasn't that cold; it was just that I wasn't warm. My suit seemed to be working quite well, considering I am sitting still in the sled. When hunting with the Inuit, they will provide you with caribou skins to supplement your personal gear. These skins are very warm, but I hadn't accepted them as I hoped my clothing would work. It's hard to generate any body heat as the only movement I have while riding in the wood sled is hanging onto the side of the sled. The ride is very rough. I wouldn't recommend this trip for someone with a bad back.

About two hours into the trip, as per Inuit tradition, we stop for tea. These guys are practically undressed as we sip tea and eat frozen raw arctic char and bread baked in a circle called bannock. I am still covered with clothing from head to foot. I undo my face mask just enough to gather in a quick bite or take a sip of tea. If the wind wasn't blowing, I think it would be quite nice. Wally is a jokester, and I am thinking that all the Inuit seem to be fun-loving with just a little prankster in them. He tells me I'm holding up pretty good for a Southerner, and he jokingly tells me the last hunter had to stop only a mile from town. God, I'm glad I didn't stop then when I thought I was cold. He also tells me this same hunter had asked to do exactly what we are doing, but after the first stop at one mile, he changed his mind and wanted to do the "town hunt." His clothing wasn't very good, and even with the caribou skins, Wally had a tough time keeping him warm. If you recall in chapter 2, I vowed to buy the best clothing I could find, and it sure seemed appropriate here. I was thinking about the dentist on the plane and wondering if he was warm.

We are traveling mostly on the sea ice as we skirt the coastline of Victoria Island. It is very beautiful, with five-hundred-foot sheer cliffs in view most of the time. I only see them occasionally as I lift my goggles, which are iced over. The sea is rough in most places as it froze when the wind was blowing, thus producing a very rough ride. We pass many muskox herds along the way, but we don't stop. I find out later that Wally could judge these animals at great distances with just his eyes.

About 2:00 p.m., I hear the engine of the snowmobile that is hooked to my sled laboring, and then it turns louder. In moments, we stop, and a discussion ensues. It seems the motor has blown up. Of course, I am immediately in panic mode as I am thinking how are we going to get back to Holman. Wally can't see my face, but I think he can tell by my body language that I am concerned. He says, "Looks like we'll have to walk back." That's not what I need to hear, but I relax as I think, *Hey, we have two snowmobiles, and they will just take me back to Holman.* However, that's not the plan. Wally says they have spare parts along and will overhaul the motor right here. I just look at him through my iced goggles and say, "Yeah right. YOU'VE GOT TO BE KIDDING." You guys are going to take this motor apart and put it back together with new parts right here at -45 degrees with the wind blowing. And that they did. They put up a tarp to block the wind, and in two hours, we were running again. They worked the whole time without gloves. I have never seen such tough people.

We arrived late in the afternoon at a small cabin that Wally and his family use during the summer for fishing. This cabin was a welcome surprise. I was expecting to be staying in the Hilton by tent. We put our gear in the cabin and had time to go and look for muskox. We found a herd, and Wally was instantly excited. The laws while hunting muskox are that once you locate a herd, you are not allowed to use the snowmobiles to pursue your quarry. Therefore, we started out on foot and tried to get in front as they moved away from us. I wasn't able to move very fast in my big boots. The herd was about a mile away with a row of small hills behind them. Wally said we should get back to the snowmobiles, get out of sight, and do a big circle behind them. Our strategy then would be to come over the hill on foot to get a look at them. This worked great, and one bull looked exceptional.

As we approached into the wind, the herd went into defensive mode. The cows made a big circle with their noses pointed outward and hid the bulls on the inside. I was thinking when I saw this about how different the human species acts, with the women and children inside. I could just hear the rumblings from the fairer human sex if they had to surround the males in time of crisis. We now were close enough to judge the size of horns. There were two bulls about the same size. Wally thought the one on the left was better because his boss looked wider. I maneuvered so as to get an open shot at the bull. It was complicated as the cows did a spectacular job of guarding their males. Maybe it really was just a case of the males knowing where to stand so as to be out of sight from the danger.

After fifteen minutes of moving back and forth, I got my shot. It was good, and the bull fell as the herd quietly moved away. It was as though they knew once the bull was down, the danger had passed. Pretty incredible! The bull was very good and well above average. I am so glad to have made the extra effort to get beyond town.

We took pictures, and Wally began the work of removing the hide for a full-size mount. They worked again without gloves. I stood, watched, and got a bit cold as I was soaked inside my parka from the walk across the tundra, but I was happy to have gotten a great animal on the first day of the hunt. The work was finished at dark. We enjoyed fresh muskox roast in the cabin and what an incredibly tasty wild game meat. I put it above all wild game I have tasted.

Wallace and myself with the "Muskie"

In the morning, we packed up for the ride back to Holman. The snowmobiles started better than I thought they would, considering the temperature was again -45 degrees. We had about 400 pounds more returning than on the trip out. We put the Polaris snow machines to the test. An overnight in Holman, and as a surprise, the plane was due back the next morning. Normally, it is only one time per week, but I was lucky the plane would be here the day I needed it.

I mentioned earlier in the chapter how impressive the village of Holman appears. Wally again was my tour guide, and he showed me the huge diesel storage tanks. The entire village gets its electricity from diesel generators. The fuel is brought in by boat in the summer. Next, the village has no sewer system because the ground is frozen all year, so one person is employed just dumping the sewer tanks year-round. The high school also had a hockey team, and I wondered who they played. They fly the team commercially to other villages and play. Wow, a pretty expensive operation for high school kids!

On the flight from Holman to Yellowknife, we landed at Coppermine and picked up a few passengers. Among them was the dentist I had met on the flight up from Yellowknife. He had had the same luck as me and got his muskox the first day. I noticed he had his hands bandaged, and I inquired. He said he had frozen his fingers, and they were turning black. I asked how that had happened. He said he was going out in the wood sled and was very cold as the clothing he brought with him had not protected him. He was about to have his guide stop when the feeling went out of his fingers, so he thought he was okay. I just said to myself, YOU'VE GOT TO BE KIDDING. At that point, his fingers were frozen, and he didn't realize the importance of getting them warm and having the feeling return. This is a huge mistake for a person who works with their hands. I was so glad I had spent the money to buy the best I could find. Thank you to Fred Gomez and Northern Outfitters for providing a great option in Arctic clothing.

By the way, Fred has the number 1 muskox in the SCI record book. With my muskox, I now have number 17 of my North American 29.

CHAPTER 13

9/11

Life as we knew it will be just a memory for the citizens of the United States. I watched and re-watched the new shows replaying the airplane crashing into the World Trade Center. Oh, how many things would be different from what normal used to be? I suspected banking would be difficult, transportation might be impossible because of fuel shortages, and airplanes might be grounded indefinitely. What I didn't understand at that moment was the strength of our leader George Bush. As the news unfolded, we learned of all the steps our president immediately took to protect our shores from any further attacks. The resolve of the American people was put to task by the world, and we showed them why this is the greatest nation on Earth. The single greatest asset we have in this country is the fact that most of us are still God-loving Christians. We came together out of love for one another and survived a monumental crisis, with very little help from the rest of the world.

I was harvesting kidney beans on the farm when the towers went down, and my immediate concern was if there were no money or monetary system, would I be paid for my products when I deliver to the grain companies? I was trying to imagine a scenario where the banks would help people extend loans or even forgive them when there was no way to repay them. Next, I thought about having enough fuel to complete the harvest. Crops had to be harvested from the fields because if war broke out, there would be a huge need for all the food we could produce. The next thought that I mulled over was really offtrack, but it was there. How were the people I knew who were out in hunting camps in remote places of Alaska, Canada, and the United States going to fare when they were relying on aircraft to them get back to civilization. Airplanes were grounded, so I hoped they all had enough supplies in the camp to keep them safe. I had a friend in the Yukon, one in British Columbia, and two in Alaska whom I knew were grounded.

Almost a year ago, I was in Bruce, South Dakota, having a few beers with my taxidermist, Don Behrns alias Burnie or Bern Dog. Burnie is one of my best friends and an excellent businessman. He had organized a hunt for ten people to hunt Quebec-Labrador caribou in Quebec, Canada, the previous year. They had a 100 percent success rate. He was able to get a greatly reduced rate for his own hunt by lining up the big group. Burnie is a fun-loving guy and is always pulling some prank on some one. I actually think his trip was free, but he called it a reduced rate. This hunt also works very well for his taxidermy business as each hunter can shoot two caribou, and Burnie gets to do the taxidermy for an extra eighteen caribou.

Our reason for the meeting in Bruce was Burnie was lining up another trip to Whale River Lodge in Quebec for September 2001. As we enjoyed our beers, he had asked me to go with the group. I have never been part of such a big group of hunters, but I thought it would be a blast. We planned the hunt to be a later hunt than the last time their group went. We were to leave South Dakota on September 14, 2001, and board a plane in Minneapolis early on the fifteenth. We had no idea that a year later, we would be facing an earth-shattering event.

It took less than an hour after the towers fell for Burnie to call me and ask what I thought about the caribou hunt that was only three days away. I said that we should remain optimistic, while deep in my heart, I thought it would require a miracle for us to be on a plane from Minneapolis to Montreal on September 15. We discussed the possibility of driving the entire distance to the camp, but there was no way because an area in Quebec was over five hundred miles long without roads. The phones were busy all day as everyone was bouncing ideas off one another on any variety of subjects. People in general were scared, but as the day wore on, everyone could see that we would not let terrorism be the downfall of the United States. During the next few days, we all waited to see what the official call out of Washington, DC, would be as to restarting air travel.

Air travel did restart within the next few days. I checked on my flight to Montreal, and I learned the flight was still scheduled just as it was originally. What great news! I'm not the smartest person in the world, but I do know that after airlines haven't flown for three days, there had to be a tremendous backlog of passengers. They needed to get somewhere in short order. How in the world could our plane be back on time? Of course, you know I had to comment to the nice reservation lady my words: "YOU'VE GOT TO BE KIDDING." Burnie and I talked and decided everyone would leave early in the morning and drive to Minneapolis on the fifteenth and we would see how the planes were doing. We could spend time there if we had major delays but would be ready when we could fly.

We arrived about 5:00 a.m. for our 7:00 a.m. flight. We hadn't even thought about the fact that we all had at least one rifle with us and we were going to board an airplane. As we unloaded our gear from the vehicle curbside at the airport, we began to wonder how this would go. My nephew, Nathan, was also going with us as part of the ten hunters. He lived in Minneapolis, so he met us at the airport in the unload zone. The idea to transport his rifle was to pack it with mine in my hard-sided gun case. We were four days after 9/11 with an open gun case curbside at the Minneapolis airport, adding Nathan's rifle to my gun case. I had no more than unsnapped the latches when a police officer started walking our way. I thought, *Here we go, we are about to find out we can't be traveling with guns.* He walked up, and I expected the words "Sir, please hand over the rifles and come with me." Instead, he was very nice and asked if we needed help. Wow, what a great country!

We had been so busy getting our gear unloaded and the vehicles parked that we hadn't noticed the complete lack of people or cars. Normal curbside at airports tends to be shoulder to shoulder and a little pushing and shoving. The place was almost empty. I am not exaggerating when I say I couldn't see a hundred people. We walked right up to the ticket counter and checked our bags with no wait. The plane to Detroit was on time as was our connecting flight to Montreal. I felt so embarrassed now about what I had said to the reservation woman that I would have liked to have called her back to apologize. It seemed that people were afraid to fly because of the attack. The plane was less than a quarter full as we headed to Detroit. We passed through Canadian customs without a wait and then boarded another almost empty plane and headed to Montreal. During the flight, we were able to move around, so we all got acquainted. We overnighted in Montreal. The outfitter met us at the hotel. We ended up at the bar in the hotel, and it seemed everyone was in a mood for kicking back and relaxing. We spent time until early morning swapping hunting stories.

The workhorse in the caribou hunting world

The topic of most interest was the question of how 9/11 had already changed our lives. We had a 5:00 a.m. flight to Central Quebec on a commercial flight. The outfitter told us to get any alcohol we needed before leaving Montreal as this was the last chance to get any. This reminded me of the brown bear hunt at Yakutat, Alaska, as I was the only one in our group to buy some beer before we left. I guess on this trip, everyone had too many spirits until too early in the morning to think about taking any alcohol along. I bought two cases of beer. This turned out great for me as I sold $3 beer for $6 at the camp. Hey, every little bit helps when trying to fill the hunting fund.

We took a very large floatplane out to the camp. A thousand-horsepower Otter can certainly haul a payload. The camp was all cabins and was more than I expected. We met Jim, who would guide the three of us. I was teamed up with Nathan and one of Burnie's friends, Kerry. Opening morning, Nathan drew first shot, so after the boat ride across the lake, we began the search for Nathan's caribou. He got his first one about an hour into the hunt. Around noon, I got my first bull. I was so thrilled as he was a very nice mature bull. He also had a double shovel, which only 5 percent of caribou have. He had a beautiful white mane, which is a sign of an older bull.

A nice double shovel

The next day, our guide, Jim, concentrated on getting Kerry his first caribou. I asked if he would mind if I took off in another direction and guided myself for the day. "Absolutely. That would be great." Away I went, but I didn't go far before I ran into a very big herd. Traveling at the end of the herd was a very good bull. I took off at an angle to try to cut him off. My plan worked great as I took one shot, and I had my second caribou. He was a little wider and heavier than the first but only had one shovel.

This was a fantastic hunt as I had my two caribou in two days. Most of the other guys had been equally successful. Burnie's son, Tucker, was on the hunt with us. What a polite young man! He connected with an unbelievable bull. Everyone was glad to see him have the success. There are so few young people starting a hunting career today, so with this caribou, it will be hard for Tucker not to continue hunting. I am an official scorer for Safari Club, and Tucker's caribou scores very high for the record book. It easily makes the Boone and Crockett minimums for entry into their record book also. Tucker handled the success very well as he didn't brag or get cocky. His father has taught him well.

Caribou number two

Nathan's second caribou was very good. He was very wide and had lots of good points. It was also great for Nathan, like Tucker, to have good success as he is also a young hunter starting out.

We had a lot of fun at this camp. There is nothing better than the conversations around the supper table when everyone is seeing and getting trophy animals. The pile of horns by the end of day number 5 had grown to be nineteen sets. One of the other hunters in our group was Donnell. He lives close to Burnie and helps him with some of the taxidermy work. Burnie uses Donnell to flesh hides and be a second set of hands when doing life size or large heads. I didn't know Donnell very well before this trip, but I know he has kept track of the progress I have made in my endeavor to take the North American 29. He has done taxidermy work on all my sheep as they are all life size. He appeared to be a little apprehensive as we started this trip together. I think his original thoughts about me were along the lines of some rich, cocky hunter with a full hunting fund and too much time on his hands, out collecting big game animals. He now appeared to have softened and took enough time to get to know me as a hunter as well as my personality. He sees that I am different than he envisioned.

Burnie and Tucker in our first class camp

Ten hunters and Nineteen horns

I can be a prankster with the best of them. Donnell is somewhat more serious than I am and pays attention to detail. It was his job to keep daily count on the horns. When a new set arrived, he would go through the whole pile to get a new count. I did something that wasn't meant to be mean, but it caused some real stress for Donnell. On day 5, we had nineteen sets of horns in the camp, but in the afternoon, Donnell came into the bunkhouse, terribly excited, and said the count was only eighteen. I looked at him seriously and said, "We better find out what's missing." He had taken two caribou, so I suggested he see if his or mine were missing. If ours were all right, we would then go through everyone's until we find whose was missing.

After an hour of counting, recounting, and looking, he realized that one of his set of horns was missing. Donnell is a great guy, but he is now worrying himself sick about his horns being gone. Twice I said to him he should count again, just to make sure. Away he went and ended with the same results every time. He finally realized the joke was on him, but no one owned up to taking his horns. Now the search of the whole camp was on as Donnell knew they had to be somewhere. I had done a good job of hiding them, so by late

146

afternoon, Donnell was frantic. While he wasn't looking, I sneaked the horns back in the pile. I suggested he count them again, which he did. He was ecstatic when the count was again nineteen. He suspected that I had done this to him, so he really did a good job of getting back at me. His caribou were very good trophies, so he said to me, "As much trophy hunting as you've done, I thought you would hold out and take great caribou." Ouch! That hurt as I thought mine were pretty good. He actually called my caribou "dinks". I deserved that and do apologize for being so mean to Donnell as he really is a great guy.

This hunt ended very successfully for everyone, and we loaded up our gear, meat, and horns and headed for Montreal. The trip home was also very quiet with mostly empty planes. It was good to get home as it was time to continue harvest. I now had eighteen species of my North American 29.

CHAPTER 14

Strike 3

Another Alaskan brown bear hunt is taking place on the Alaskan Peninsula, and I am on it. It is 33 degrees, windy, and raining. I am chilled to the bone. My guide, Tim Garbe, and I have been standing in the rain on the top of this little mountain for over six hours. We hoped we might catch a glimpse of a big Alaskan brown bear, but no luck today. Tim has told me repeatedly it is futile to think we will see any bears out roaming around in this kind of weather. Of course, I have not listened to his advice, and I don't know why I haven't because I do believe that the guide is always right. He really is telling me in a nice way that the bears are acting more intelligently than we are. At least they are under cover, waiting for a sunny day. Really, it isn't right that Tim suffers these conditions just to appease me, but as this chapter unfolds, you will see the reason for my insanity.

A tremendous amount of change had taken place for Becky and me in the previous few months. You have heard me talk of the hunting fund in previous chapters as being on zero or lower. Well, that was about to change. The farm in South Dakota that we loved and nurtured since 1980 is now part of our history. Some of our neighbors approached us with an offer to buy that we couldn't refuse. Becky and I paid far too much for this farm in 1980, and we had a pact. When we could recoup our investment plus a little profit, we were going to accept an offer. The sale took place in February 2004. The decision to sell was not easy, and we suffered seller's remorse. We now had enough money to replenish the hunting fund so I could finish collecting the North American 29. We also spent time in

Phoenix after the transaction and decided we would build a winter home away from the cold and snow of South Dakota.

It is May 2004, and I am very familiar with the area we are currently hunting. Today is day 11, and I am remembering this scenery as I was here at the very same spot last October. I had spent twelve days last fall doing the same thing we have done today. We leave our tent a little before daybreak, cross over a wide river valley, and then climb to the top of this small mountain. I am in better shape now than when the hunt began, and we have taken almost a half hour off the climb since day 1. We stay put on the mountain most of the day, glassing for bears as we can see up and down a large valley. Tim says you don't go wondering around in bear country. Everywhere you walk, you leave your scent. We witnessed firsthand what can happen with our scent and the bears. A few days before, we watched a bear that was too small to hunt walk up to the track we follow across the valley every day, sniff it, and then turn 180 degrees and walk back right where he came from. Thus, we have been very careful not to put any more scent out than is necessary. We stalked one bear early in the hunt that looked big enough from afar, but he was too small when we got to him. It's too bad as we left our scent over quite a few miles of terrain.

Another raining day while brown bear hunting

I could have been the weatherman thus far on this trip and on the last bear hunt. My prediction for the weather tomorrow is rain and more rain. I do like rain because as a farmer, my livelihood is determined by the amount of rain we get. If we get enough rain, I can usually pay the banker back at the end of the year, and in the rare event we get a little extra rain, I can then replenish the hunting fund. If you recall in 2002, we experienced a terrible drought. I would have given anything that year just to have a few sprinkles. Now I find myself cussing the rain daily. You may also recall in chapter 8, the last four days of my brown bear hunt in Yakutat, Alaska, were turned into "sit-in-camp days" because of the deluge we received. With this being day number 11 of this hunt, twelve days of hunting brown bear last October and eight days of hunting in September 1996 in Yakutat, I now have a total of thirty-one days of brown bear hunting. Of these, during the last twenty-seven, it has rained most of the time. All I can say is "YOU'VE GOT TO BE KIDDING."

This is my third try at getting one of these beautiful creatures. Thus far, in my endeavor to take the "North American 29," I have enjoyed more success than I probably deserve. In almost all my hunts, I have taken the animal I sought on the first try, and they have all been better than average in trophy size. Most have been way above average. The Lord has definitely taken care of me, but I'm not sure of His plans for me while hunting brown bear. I am certainly being put to a test. It is not that I hadn't seen any bears; I just couldn't find one big enough. In Yakutat, I saw thirty-three bears, and here at Stepovak Bay on the peninsula, I have seen over one hundred bears.

Tomorrow will be the last day of this hunt, but I am very optimistic. I have done very well on the last day of different hunts. I think back to the pure luck in chapter 8 in which I got my Coues deer in the last hour of the last day. I never give up, and this attitude has kept my relationship with my guides very good. I think they have appreciated the fact that I am always pleasant, even though things may not be going so well. Okay, you are right, I'm not that perfect, but I talk a good story. It's not always easy when trophy hunting to remain upbeat, and on this hunt, I really was beginning to be a whiner. I didn't like that, but try as I might otherwise, I was just plain grumpy.

Thus, we are standing all day in the cold rain, even though my guide says we will not have any luck. As I said earlier, I wasn't being fair to Tim as it wasn't his fault that it rained incessantly.

Looking out to the Pacific, we almost saw the sun this day

You have heard me talk of my hunting fund in previous chapters. My emotions are further complicated on this hunt because the fund is not empty for brown bear, but I have spent too much in the pursuit of a big bear. The cost for the three hunts is over $35,000. This doesn't include the cost of airline flights to Anchorage and hunting licenses. The sale of part of our farm provided relief for the empty hunting fund. I still had to be somewhat lucky in my hunting. It's no wonder that before I left home, Becky had very seriously told me there would be no more brown bear hunts after this one. It was hard to tell Becky that I had seen a great number of bears, but I hadn't brought one home. If I was unsuccessful this time, it would be strike 3, and you are out.

I think you can get a sense of my insistence that we hunt when conditions are less than ideal. I wanted to take a bear so badly that I made Tim suffer with me. It was looking very poorly for the home team on this, day 11, but in hunting, things can change very rapidly.

Thinking back to last October, on the last day of the hunt, we had decided we would check out some new territory around a small lake. Dick Lounsbury, who has been my outfitter for these past two brown bear hunts, had seen a big bear while flying another hunter to his camp. He flew us out the evening before the last day and set up camp about two miles from the lake. I was thrilled with this new camp and my new guide, Tim Garbe. The tent was a twelve feet square instead of the seven-footer I had just come from, and it had a tall ceiling. This size was needed as I was now hunting with a guy who was six feet six inches, and he needed a tall tent. I could stand in this tent, making it very easy to get dressed in the morning.

Tim is a firefighter in Anchorage and is Dick's most successful guide. He had just finished getting a huge bear for another hunter. The reason he was helping me instead of the guide I started with was that back on day number 5, my original guide had broken his ankle. We were coming down a rather steep mountain after putting a stalk on a bear that turned out to be too small. He had slipped on some loose shale, and his foot got caught underneath and snapped his ankle.

He was very valiant as he made the extremely painful trip back to our tent. That night was the only time I feared for my life on any of my bear hunts. The location we were hunting on the Alaskan Peninsula was a pretty narrow strip of land with huge mountains filled with glaciers. It was located between the Bering Sea to the north and the Pacific Ocean to the south. There were times when a storm moved across from the north, got on the downslope of the huge mountains, and produced winds in excess of 100 miles per hour.

This was exactly what happened this night. The winds were unbelievable, the tent was practically leaving with us inside, it was 33 degrees, and it was pouring rain. My guide being injured only worsened an already bad situation. All I could do was pray and think, YOU'VE GOT TO BE KIDDING. I thought South Dakota was windy, but this was crazy. If the tent were to uproot and take off in the wind, we would surely die from hypothermia. I would have felt a little safer if my guide was at 100 percent.

The scenario with a laid-up guide had somewhat crippled my chances to get a bear. They came with the Super Cub and flew me back to the base camp. My hunt then had become a walk from the base camp out to bear country. The trip took six hours one way, and then we would return to the camp. We were crossing a lot of very open territory filled with about six inches of water everywhere. We hadn't seen any bears. To be able to go to an actual spike camp again and have Tim as a guide on the last day made so happy.

Tim and I awoke on the morning of the last day of last fall's hunt to an overcast day with only a light sprinkle instead of steady rain. We headed out toward the lake where the bear had been seen, and after a two-hour hike, we spot the bear fishing on the far end of the lake. It looked like he was moving our way, but he was in the water. Sure enough, by eleven o'clock, he was within one hundred yards of us with just his head showing above the water. He was a very nice bear, and I would be thrilled to have him. I was thinking this was great, and I prepared to take a shot. That was when I heard Tim telling me not to shoot. I said, "What do you mean don't shoot?" Tim asked, "If you shoot him in the water, how are we going to get him out?" I hadn't thought about that, but YOU'VE GOT TO BE KIDDING.

I tried to reason with Tim that we surely could wade into the lake, tie a rope around the bear, and pull him to shore. I also mentioned we could build a raft, float out, and get him back to shore on the raft. I couldn't come up with a scenario that Tim liked, so I never fired a shot. Tim said our best chance was to try to figure out where the bear might exit the lake and set up an ambush. We tried to move quietly around the lake to get to where the bear had gone into the water, but the bear had his own ideas and chose to leave the water almost 180 degrees away from us. When he got to shore, I had time for one quick offhand shot at a running bear. I wanted to get a rest, but there wasn't time or anything available. I missed the shot, and the bear ran up the mountain. We pursued, thinking we might catch a glimpse as we reached the top, but the bear had hiked the mountain in just a few minutes, while it took us an hour to the top. We never saw him again. That ended the last day of my second unsuccessful Alaskan brown bear hunt. I was disappointed, but I told myself I would try again.

This brings us back to day 11 in May 2004. The day has ended without a bear. Tim has taken quite a few bears in the area we are glassing. He says they come out of their den at the top of the mountains and make the long trek through the snow to get down to the valley. During the day, they rest, and toward evening, they start walking across the big valley in front of us, ending up on the mountain where we are located. Then the hunter works his way down to get a shot, and the hunt is successful. Sounds too good to be true, especially when dealing with wild animals, doesn't it? Thus far, in eleven days of hunting here, our bear has not appeared. I guess he must still be sleeping. I am having a real hard time with this story, but Tim assures me it has happened exactly this way more than once.

Okay, I can play along with a good story as well as anyone, so this being the last day, I will wait it out and see if it will happen today. We make our usual walk across the valley from the tent, climb our little mountain, and start glassing. You won't believe this, but sure enough, about 10:00 a.m., a bear appears at the top of the mountain across the valley. He is very high up and appears to be right next to the glaciers. He is moving very slowly, and Tim says he has just emerged from the den. If this bear does as Tim has predicted, his next move will be to slowly work his way down the mountain and spend the afternoon in the alders at the bottom. I can't believe what I am seeing as he does exactly that. Now it's time for a "YOU'VE GOT TO BE KIDDING."

The bear disappears about 2:00 p.m., and Tim says he is just lying down in the alders as he has become too hot because of the difference in elevation he has seen in the past few hours. The next hours are excruciatingly painful as we wait in hope of seeing the bear again. Oh, by the way, this is the biggest bear I have seen in three trips, so I am so excited. I don't care if he is a world record or not; he is well above average and exceeds my goals. I would be happy to get a chance to get him. It gets dark now about 11:30 p.m., so we have a few hours before our quarry needs to make a move. At around 8:00 p.m., we see him again. He is exactly where we lost sight of him earlier in the afternoon; thus, Tim was right again about the bear just lying down to cool off. At this point, he is about two miles away and is just milling around. I am praying that he proves Tim correct and starts to cross the valley and head to our mountain. I have a strange feeling that this is about to happen. I will gladly give Tim his due credit if his prediction comes true.

As we wait, Tim lets me in on another bit of information that could be useful. He says if the bear does come across the valley, we have to make a decision on which end of our mountain he will go. It seems that at almost the last minute, we go one way and hope that we choose correctly. This only adds to the number of things that will need to happen in the next few hours if we are to be successful.

Here he comes! Almost as if on cue, the big bear starts out across the river valley. He is not moving fast but at least at a steady pace. There are so many places he could simply turn and walk, and we would not see him again. During those times when he is out of sight for a few minutes, pessimism takes control of my brain. His pace takes him about halfway across in an hour. I now calculate that at the current pace, he will reach the mountain about 10:00 p.m. I ask Tim how long it would take to get from our spot to the end of the farthest end of the mountain. He says about forty-five minutes of hard running.

Oh boy, if this is to happen, we will have just enough time before dark. I am totally optimistic as I really do believe it is going to happen exactly as Tim said it would.

It's amazing that "Old Brownie" isn't even stopping to eat or anything. He appears to be on a mission. This is absolutely incredible now as he is almost to our side of the valley. It is 10:15 p.m., and Tim says, "Get your gear. We are going." "That's easy," I say. I've been ready for three hours. I've had my pack on my back, just waiting for the word "go." Tim figures we better go to the west end of the mountain and then work our way down to meet the bear. We take off running, and I soon find how far behind a six-foot-six-inch guide I can be in a short time.

We cross a huge alder patch with trees about four feet tall. Alder trees are notorious for being impossible to traverse, and these are complicated by the fact they are full of snow. I am doing more tugging and pulling versus running because either I am always stuck in the snow or hooked on the alder branches. Tim seems to be able to go faster, but he is kind enough not to laugh too much at the sight of me trying my hardest. In fifteen minutes, I am drenched in sweat, but I don't want to waste the time to undress. Finally, we emerge to the part of the mountain with no alders, but it is extremely steep. I guess that's why there are no alders as they tend to grow on more of the flat surfaces. Now I am tumbling, sliding, rolling, and slipping on the snow and totally exhausted. This short hike we are on may be the most humiliating stalk I have ever put on an animal. I am not in control but see the urgency to get where we are going.

The huge landscape "Old Brownie" covered to get to our mountain

Tim stops suddenly and explains that we should be able to see the bear from the vantage point we now have. He is nowhere to be seen.

Tim thinks that after we left the top, the bear decided to go around the east end. My heart sinks as it is now 10:55 p.m., and the chances of us getting to the bear before dark are now impossible. We sit for a minute, which allows me to catch my breath. I quickly check my rifle to make sure everything is okay as I have never taken so many tumbles in my hunting career as I have in the last half hour.

I look through the scope, and I can see nothing but blue. Okay, I think, I have snow on the end, and its blocking the light. Nope, the scope is clean, but I can't see through it. "God," I say, "YOU'VE GOT TO BE KIDDING." I can't find the words to tell Tim at this point. I don't know what to say. He is now busy deciding if there is some route that may enable us to get to the bear before dark. I can see on his face that look that says, "I'm sorry, but there is no chance of success." We certainly have given it our best, but it didn't work. It's funny in life how things can be so fleeting. Tim and I both kind of let out a sigh and slump to the ground about the same time.

At the same time, "Old Brownie" appears no less than 250 yards below us, and he is a big bear. He must have been stopped in the alders while we were discussing our plan. He surely must have heard some of our conversation. We are both too excited to speak and kind of scramble to our feet, looking to see what the bear would do next. In our excitement, I had forgotten about the huge problem with my Zeiss scope. I knew I had to tell Tim, but I was almost in tears when I thought about how hard we had worked to get here, not to mention all the days I had made him suffer in the cold rain, and now we may not get a shot at this bear. "Tim," I said, "I have a huge problem." Before I could finish, he said, "What, are you scared, or you have to go to the bathroom, right?" I say, "No, neither of those. I can't see anything through my scope!"

You should have seen the look on his face. I was almost afraid for the bear because I think if he had been close, I would have witnessed a man kill a bear with his bare hands. After he got over the shock, he took my rifle and looked through the scope. He determined that if you had the barrel pointed to the ground and then quickly raised it to your shoulder for a shot, there was a second or so that a little ring on the outside of the glass was clear enough to see a sliver of a target. We are not sure if the scope will work, but our plan is to get within two hundred yards of the bear and have the barrel down. When I am ready for a shot, I will raise the rifle quickly, get on the bear's front shoulder, and fire.

Therefore, we climb just a little lower, and from a sitting position, I tried our plan a couple of times without firing the Weatherby. It seemed like it could work. I needed a few seconds for a short prayer to ask God to help my equipment work the best it could under the circumstances. The daylight is almost gone, so we have to try immediately. The bear emerged from a small depression and stood almost broadside at two hundred yards. I quickly raised the rifle and shot. I have never fired that quickly in my life, even at a running target. The shot was good, and the bear crumbled into a pile in the alders. It looks like the one shot will be enough. Wow, I am so thrilled, and I thank Tim. It's incredible that this scenario played exactly as Tim said. I give him his credit.

"Old Brownie"

What a relief! We wanted to wait a few minutes before we headed for a closer look. It is 11:35 p.m., and our light is gone, so we go right away. As I cautiously approach, I can tell he is indeed a good bear. As usual, I have to get teary-eyed and thank God for a remarkable day. The bear remains down, and after a few pictures and high fives, we head for the camp.

I honestly could have stayed right there as I was mentally and physically exhausted. The trip to our tent took an extra two hours as we had gotten farther away from it when we took off to the west from the top of our mountain.

I couldn't sleep when I got back to the tent. I was reliving all the details of this hunt and the previous two brown bear hunts. Tim is certainly my newest hero. His patience and willingness to put up with my fickle nature has provided a wonderful trophy. Finally getting my brown bear puts my North American 29 at 19.

CHAPTER 15

The New Classification

This chapter and the short narrative in chapter 1 are the only ones in this book that contain some material that is out of chronological order. Thus far, these writings since chapter 2 have taken you from my number 1 species and moved forward as each species was collected. In this chapter, it is easier to include all my black bear hunts instead of writing about them separately and placing them in the proper order. Safari Club International (SCI) was looking at entries in their record books of North American animals and noticed the black bears coming from the islands in the Canadian Pacific Ocean were scoring much higher than their cousins were from the mainland in North America. They determined they would make a new classification for bears called the Coastal (Pacific) or island bear. The black bears taken on the mainland would now be called continental black bears. This happened after I had taken two black bears. You will see how this new classification actually shortened the number of hunts I needed to complete my North American 29.

In the last chapter, I introduced Dick Lounsbury. He was the outfitter I had hunted with twice for Alaskan brown bear. He felt badly about the incident in October 2003 when my guide got hurt and put a halt to my success for that brown bear hunt. He was unable to discount the second hunt in May 2004 because of the fees he had to pay the natives down on the Alaskan Peninsula just to operate a camp there. His solution was to offer me a chance to hunt black bear free on some property he owned northwest of Anchorage, Alaska. After taking my brown bear in May of 2004, I said yes to his offer to hunt his property around Beluga Mountain.

Becky and I had gone to Minnesota a few years earlier and hunted black bear. Brian Bachman had provided a very good hunt, but we were unsuccessful in collecting a bear. We did get to see a very funny story unfold though. The first day in our very beautiful base

Becky at the bear lodge in Minnesota

camp, we met a young man who was a very accomplished archer. He had just won a major international shooting contest. He had joined us to hunt bear, and he was practicing his shooting in the afternoon before we set out to the stands for the evening hunt. His arrows were hitting bull's-eye from 110 yards. I am not an archer, but I do know this is outstanding, and all Becky and I could say was "YOU'VE GOT TO BE KIDDING." He had a film crew with him, and they were going to film him hunting this evening. Becky and I went to our stand, and they went their separate way.

After dark, all the hunters were gathered around the supper table at the lodge, and the film crew set up to show the group the action the young archer had encountered a few hours earlier. A bear had come to his bait station and stood about 20 yards away. An arrow flew and missed its target. The bear made a quick retreat to the woods but was back at the bait in about fifteen minutes, and the scenario repeated itself with a missed shot. It happened a third time, and this young man could not have been more embarrassed. There were very few of us who have not had a little "buck fever." He was very humbled, and I'm sure this is a lesson he will never forget.

Becky joined me on the trip to Anchorage in August 2004. We were hoping to have a better "couple's retreat" than the trip to British Columbia in 2000. The flight to Anchorage was great, and Dick was going to fly us across the Knik Arm to his cabin near the mountain. He is a dealer for Maule airplanes, so we all got to fly at the same time as these bush planes hold four people. What a great concept for a bush plane versus the old standby, the Super Cub. I don't think Becky enjoyed the ride as much as I did as she has never been a very good flier. I mentioned earlier in the book that I have a private pilot's license, but I never was able to get Becky to fly with me if I was the pilot. This didn't bother me as I wouldn't have wanted something happening to both of us in the same accident because of our kids and family.

We spent six days hunting. It was a lot of fun and were together the entire time. The temperatures were in the nineties every day, which is very abnormal for Alaska. We got out in the woods at daybreak and left a little before dark to return to the cabin. A little humor here that we hurt our chances at bigger bears as Becky just would not stay past dark in any area that had bears, so we were always out of the bear habitat before dark. We did take a small bear that Becky thought was a monster before the shot. She learned the valuable lesson that inflicts hunters of all ages, which is "ground shrinkage." The bear was about a six feet square, and we were thrilled to be able to be together to see the hunt to the finish. It was during the skinning process of this bear that created the health problems for me that you will read about in the next chapter. I now had my number 20 species, and it seemed like a great milestone. I was over two-thirds done now with the North American 29.

As this chapter started, I said the chronological order of this book will be altered here. The bear I took in Alaska was just not the size needed to achieve the goals I set for myself. I wanted to get a larger bear. Most hunters know the biggest black bears come from places like Vancouver Island, British Columbia, or the smaller islands in the

The black bear from Beluga Mountain

Pacific like the Queen Charlotte, the ABC, or Prince of Wales. My idea was to book a hunt to take one of these larger bears.

Looking across rhe Pacific Ocean towards Queen Charlotte Island

After talking with John Gates and Blair Worldwide Hunting, I booked with Prophet Muskwa, which is by Kevin Olmsted. The hunt was to take place on Queen Charlotte Islands, British Columbia, during October 2005. As you will read in the next chapters, I actually took three additional species between these two black bear hunts, thus the break in the chronological order. It just makes more sense to combine these two.

My brother Steve had taken a number of black bears in Saskatchewan, including a few different color phases. He was also interested in a chance to take a larger bear, so he made the decision to join me on the hunt. The trip to Vancouver was great, but we arrived too late to get to Queen Charlotte the same day. The overnight in Vancouver was great as we caught up on all our newly planned hunting trips and reminisced about all the old ones.

The short two-hour flight to the islands and the ferry ride to another island went perfectly. The lodge and our guides were incredible. We learned that next day we would use spot-and-stalk technique to hunt these bears. The first day went by without any bears, but our guides soon discovered the competitive spirit between two brothers. The next day, we saw bears, but they were too small.

On day 3, we had some real fun. My guide and I were traveling down a very well used logging road, and there he stood. He was only two hundred yards off the road, looking at us as we drove by. My guide said we would just continue driving until out of sight, very quietly stop, and get out of the truck. We proceeded to walk back up the road and look for the bear. He had gone back to eating berries, and I got in a position for a shot. One shot and the hunt was over. I have never had an easier stalk, and I thanked God for the opportunity to be here in this place at this time. I should have yelled at the top of my lungs before the shot I took "YOU'VE GOT TO BE KIDDING!" I didn't do it, but how could it be any easier? I sat thinking about how for once my procrastination to get in great physical shape hadn't hurt me.

The new classification: the island bear

The picture taking proved to be a challenge as this bear weighed about 600 pounds and had fallen in some terrible down timber. We couldn't move him except to get his front paws over the log in front of him. We got the pictures we could and skinned for a life-size mount and headed back to the camp. It was dark when we arrived, and we got the news from Steve that he had taken his bear in the morning. At this point, we didn't let anyone know that I had my bear. We just celebrated Steve being done with his hunt. After supper, I asked Steve if we could measure his hide to see how good he had done. It measured seven feet and two inches square. That is huge, and I just had to say "YOU'VE GOT TO BE KIDDING." I have never seen a bigger black bear.

The new classification: The island bear

We couldn't move him from this hole to get better pictures

Steve's bear on the right

After seeing how much Steve's bear measured, I didn't even want to let him know I had gotten mine. It would be hard to admit defeat in our competition. A few more beers and my guide let the news slip that I had also taken a bear. Now the celebrating moved to the next level, and everyone except me was anxious to do some more measuring. We laid the bears out next to each other, and they looked the same size. The tape put mine an inch bigger at the start, but I think the guide may have unfairly stretched the hide. We ended with the same size bears, so no one had bragging rights, but they were both so much bigger than average that we could have cared less.

What an incredible experience and coincidence that we would take these on the same day. Steve had also gotten his from the road. They had gotten out of the truck to drain some morning coffee, and the bear crossed the road behind them. His guide had just gotten done telling him to be prepared as bears often cross the road after the truck goes by. Sure enough, the story came true, but Steve was prepared and took him with one shot.

The beautiful Queen Charlotte Islands

The interesting part of this entire story is sometime a year later, SCI decided to add these "island" bears as a different species. This decision on their part gave me my twenty-fourth species. I couldn't have been happier as all I did was try to get a bigger bear, and it ended being another species. This scenario was so welcome as it saved me an entire hunt to get finished with the North American 29. How could it get any better or luckier than this?

CHAPTER 16

Homecoming

Our son Kiel (pronounced Kyle) came to us in the fall of 1999 with an announcement. He was to graduate from high school in May of 2000. He told us he wanted to join the marines upon graduation. This was quite a shock for Becky and I. Kiel had been involved with us on the farm his entire life, so we assumed he would go to college and then return to the farm. Of course, we played devil's advocate with Kiel, but we could see he had his mind made up. He has always been a very conservative person with a love of our great country, and he wanted to go and serve his country. How could we argue with that kind of commitment?

In July 2000, we said goodbye as Kiel headed to San Diego for three months of marine boot camp. We were not allowed any contact with him during this period except for mail. Becky and I tried to write a letter a day to encourage him. He is a very strong person and would have made it through the training easily without our support. The day of his graduation, we were there in San Diego to attend the ceremony. If you've never been to a marine boot camp graduation, you need to put it on your "bucket list." I was in tears as we watched these young men march with such precision. They were all in excellent shape, and as they were dismissed, you could literally feel the electricity in the air as the hats went up in a big "hooray."

As a graduation gift for Kiel and as a thank-you for four years of service for the United States, we booked a caribou hunt for him. I needed a Central Canadian barren ground caribou, and I thought as long as I was going to the Northwest Territories, Canada, why not

169

include him in the hunt? We scheduled it for late summer 2004. We were going to hunt with Adventures Northwest out of Yellowknife.

Kiel had done white-tailed deer hunting on the farm; goose hunting along the Missouri River around Pierre, South Dakota; and lots of pheasant hunting around Spink County, South Dakota. This was the extent of his hunting, so the idea of going after some new animal was exciting for both of us. We talked about the trip quite a few times, and I kept teasing him about his ability to shoot. He just laughed and fired right back that I would be the one having problems shooting and his caribou would be much bigger than mine.

My teasing didn't have a chance as one of Kiel's jobs as a marine was to teach other marines how to shoot rifle and pistol. It seems his superiors found out early that Kiel was an excellent marksman. He was given the job of teaching those who couldn't pass the yearly test for marine marksmanship. The marines take their shooting ability very seriously, and if you don't pass your yearly qualification, you will be discharged. So most of the time, Kiel was teaching breathing techniques and trigger squeeze to those much higher in command than his grade. For those who would listen to Kiel, they did very well, but some of his superiors had a hard time listening to the young teacher. I felt really good about Kiel's shooting, and he proved himself at the shooting range in South Dakota before we left for Canada. He was using my .270 Weatherby Lazermark IV, and his first shot at one hundred yards was a perfect 2.8 inches high and dead center. This is perfect for this rifle. I just said to him, "YOU'VE GOT TO BE KIDDING."

He had spent his four years with the marines in Hawaii and arrived back in South Dakota in June 2004. He had time to help us on the farm that summer. I could see a wonderful change in his attitude toward his parents. Gone were the arguments on just about every subject and present was a great respect for his elders. He still had his good-natured ability to tease and have fun. We were glad to have him around to watch the farm because in August, Becky and I took a trip to Anchorage to visit Dick Lounsbury. He was, if you recall, the outfitter for two of my trips to Alaska to hunt Alaskan brown bear. He invited us to come and visit him in Anchorage. We did a black bear hunt in and around Beluga Mountain, which is northwest of Anchorage, where he kept a private cabin. Dick is also a dealer for the Maule aircraft, so we enjoyed riding in a bush plane that hauled four people instead of two like the Super Cub.

We ended up taking a midsize bear, and during the skinning process, I got a part of the bear lodged in my thumb. It got infected, and it kept growing in size. I knew that eventually, I would need treatment, but we were running day and night planting winter wheat in Texas, so I didn't take the time to take care of my thumb properly.

Floatplane airport in Yellowknife

In September, we left for Yellowknife. I was so proud to be taking along a young man who had just served our country. We overnighted in Yellowknife, but the outfitter had to take me to the emergency room to handle my thumb, which had grown to the size of a golf ball. It was just in time as the pain was more than I could stand. They got me fixed up, but as usual, Kiel had a smart remark about how I would use my sore thumb as an excuse for poor shooting. I just smirked as I thought shooting hasn't been a problem in my hunting up to this point. In the morning, we took a beautiful floatplane, a

171

1,000 horsepower Otter, to Little Martin Lake. We were a long way north of the tree line.

The camp was perfect, and we had our own cabin. Our camp cook, Dave, was a wonderful man who owned three high-end steak houses in Calgary. Needless to say, the meals were exquisite. We met our guide who was about Kiel's age, and as they visited, I could see Kiel would be very comfortable with the big game hunting scene. We learned the plan would be to take a small boat with a 15 horsepower motor across the lake and hunt away from the camp. There were eight other hunters in the camp, and we would all go our separate ways across the lake. The caribou were migrating in good numbers, so our timing was good.

Kiel and I with his caribou

On the other side of the lake, we left the boat and began covering the many miles it sometimes takes to find good bulls, even though you are up to your ears in caribou. Now I've talked a few times in this book about guides. This trip will not be an exception as our young guide was very fit, and my now ex-marine son was probably even in better shape. Therefore, that leaves the overweight farmer trying to keep up with not one guide but two. At one time, they tried to be funny, and after waiting a short time, and I mean a very short time, to catch up to them, they asked if the old man needed a "walker." Very funny, guys!

The fun is about to begin. Hunting with someone very close to you is usually very exciting. Kiel is very competitive, much like his father, so of course, this would be a competition to see who would get the biggest caribou. We each had two tags, so if we screwed up and shot something small, we could still redeem ourselves with the second tag. As he is my son, I told Kiel he could have first choice. He really does understand trophy hunting, so the first day, we never fired a shot. About noon on day 2, we came across a very good bull, and Kiel decided he would take him. Of course, it required only one shot. The caribou was very good, and there was no ground shrinkage. After many great pictures, we got the caribou back to the boat. We had only a short amount of time to finish the day, so I would have to wait for the next one.

Day number 3 produced a lot of caribou but no shooters. Day 4 was a very ugly day with wind and some rain. It reminded me of South Dakota weather as we seldom get a day without at least a 20 mph breeze. The challenge was crossing the lake in the morning. The waves were bigger than we liked, and we were wet by the time we got to the other side. The scary part was returning that evening as we were going against the wind, and 15 horsepower is not enough in these conditions. It took us over two hours to cross versus the one hour in normal conditions. I said more than one prayer as I was more nervous in this situation than in some places where I had hunted mountain sheep among sheer cliffs. I really didn't think we would survive if the boat capsized. The water is 33 degrees, and there is no rescue equipment within hundreds of miles. You might last a few hours at best in these circumstances. God heard our prayers, and we made it.

Day 5 turned out very nice, and we were seeing a lot of caribou. There were some very good bulls, and I probably should have taken one. My son made the comment, "Dad, you aren't going to take one unless it's very big, are you?" I said, "You've got that right." However, on day 5,

I did take my caribou. Now this is embarrassing as I took three shots. The first one knocked him down, and I shot again to finish him. I'm sure he was done, but the guide said shoot again, so I did. Now you guessed it. Kiel was laying it on pretty thick about my shooting ability. He said, "I suppose it's your sore thumb." It's funny how it had to be this hunt that I didn't connect in only one shot. Again, that guy Murphy had done his job making sure I would be embarrassed in front of Kiel. My caribou ended up a little bigger, so it made up for my shooting. I could just see Kiel thinking, YOU'VE GOT TO BE KIDDING.

The three shot caribou

We had two days left to hunt, so it was Kiel's turn to have choice. We looked at quite a few good bulls. I was very proud of my son as late on day 6, we had a bull that was almost identical to the one he got on day 2. We analyzed that it didn't make much sense to take him. He wasn't big enough to have bragging rights, and it would cost Kiel a $1,000 to get it home and pay the taxidermist for the mount. He passed on a couple more bulls, and we could see our young native guide was getting frustrated with us for not taking another bull. So we experienced a memory flashback to chapter 7 when José, who was guiding me for Coues deer, wouldn't hunt with me anymore.

Well, the same thing happened here. Our guide wouldn't take us out anymore. Kiel and I thought it was our choice if we took another caribou or not. I'm not sure our guide understood the trophy animal concept. At this point, both of us said, "YOU'VE GOT TO BE KIDDING."

Kiel and I with my caribou

The camp at Little Martin Lake

The hunt ended, and the next morning, we had snow, and the lake was starting to freeze over. We hoped the Otter would be able to pick us up. The weather cleared in the afternoon, and we were able to get back to Yellowknife. We enjoyed a night of visiting with our newfound friends from Minnesota. What a wonderful experience to be able to hunt with family!

CHAPTER 17

One And A Quarter Tons

"You've got to shoot lower and farther forward." I have heard this twice now, and my Irish is about ready to take over the situation. If this happens again, it won't be a pretty sight. Then the words echo again: "lower and farther forward." Six shots from my .300 Weatherby have failed to bring down my target. I am frustrated and continue to think, YOU'VE GOT TO BE KIDDING. My rifle holds three shells, and this marks the first time I have needed to reload my rifle with shells while trying to take down any of the North American 29. It's bad enough to consider having to reload once, but I am about to load in my third set of shells.

It is the middle of November, and soybean and corn harvest ran three weeks behind, so I was late getting to this hunt. I was scheduled to be here in the middle of October but just couldn't get to a level of completion of harvest I was comfortable with. You have to have a proper mind-set before deciding to just take off with crops left in the field. Over the years, I have taken off to go hunting with lots of crop left to harvest. This year, we just couldn't put a string of days together as it was either rain or mechanical breakdowns. I hate the latter because there are more important things to do at harvest than work on the equipment. However, it happens, and you do what you must.

My tardiness has usually not worked in my favor during my hunting career. In chapter 4, I was late getting started on my Stone sheep hunt. The hunt was scheduled to be fourteen days, but I missed the first four and consequently ran out of regular days without taking a ram. It was only because of the goodness of Darwin Carey in allowing me to stay an extra day that I took the beautiful forty-and-a-half-inch ram. I was hoping this wouldn't be the time for a hunt to be unsuccessful because of poor timing. A few times while hunting elk in Colorado, we were snowed out because we had gone too late in the year.

As the time for the hunt approached, I kept in touch with Dale Tingley, who was the outfitter. He said they had quite a few hunters, and most of them were scheduled about the same time as my original hunt or just a few days later. As our harvest continued and I was still in South Dakota, I called Dale almost daily to get an update on the bulls being taken. He would tell me how the hunters were taking some pretty great animals. I was probably on my tenth call before I realized what was happening. I was always excited to hear the results for the day, and then it occurred to me that every one of these great bulls that were being taken was one less that I would have a chance at getting. It's funny how the mind works sometimes. It was as if I were there and had some interest in the other hunters' animals. Now that is crazy thinking. I stopped checking with Dale and pushed the harvest as hard as I could.

Finally, the departure day arrived. I had decided early on that I would drive to Saskatchewan. The airline flight schedule wasn't the greatest, and I thought this hunt would be one of those where you get in and out rather quickly. I was thinking one day of hunting. After all, how hard can it be to find an animal as large as an American bison?

I love to drive, especially long trips. During my childhood, our family went on a great number of long trips as we had relatives in Ohio, Montana, and Minnesota. In the old days when families traveled, there was no such thing as stopping along the way for lunch or supper. The few stops were to refuel or bathroom breaks, which were sometimes quite often when traveling with six young kids in the car. I can remember my father's words very plainly. He would say "Is everyone sure they don't need to use the bathroom?" We would all shake our heads, and he would take off down the highway. Usually, he wouldn't make ten miles until someone would need some relief. I'm sure he was thinking to himself, YOU'VE GOT TO BE KIDDING. He was always good-natured about letting us out along the side of the road to use the outdoor facilities. What a great guy!

As mentioned above, we would not stop to eat. My mother would pack food for us to eat on the road. To this day, I still love a good bologna sandwich. There really is something about a sandwich tasting better when someone else makes it. Mother brought along enough food to feed us for a week, even though the trip might only be fifteen hours. The funniest part of all this is in the fact that we were begging to eat within a few miles of leaving home. I guess that was why we needed so much food.

The drive from South Dakota to Regina, Saskatchewan, takes a good twelve hours. I didn't pack lunch as my mother did because of my diet Pepsi habit. When you drink a lot of forty-four-ounce sodas, you often need the bathroom. I always had the opportunity to get something to eat as I would stop every hour. What a difference in habits a generation can make.

I arrived at the hunting camp around noon. Since I had driven instead of flying, I would be able to hunt the same day. Dale Tingley was a very gracious host, and I was staying at the ranch headquarters. Already in the camp were four elk hunters from California. They were excited as they had already seen some phenomenal elk. Also, a fine gentleman from New York had been in the camp for a few days. He explained to me that he had "elk fever" and had taken many elk over the years but had come to hunt with Dale because of his reputation for large bull elk. I was to be the only American bison hunter in the camp.

Visiting with Dale was very pleasant as he had a very refined demeanor. I could tell immediately that he was very well educated and seemed to know more about the political goings-on in the United States than I did. But this is not at all unusual in Canada as the people in general are very knowledgeable about our political system and love to converse about it. We talked about President Bush, and Dale said that he liked him. That was great with me as I am a conservative and had voted for President Bush. I have found that overall, the Western Canadian provinces are much like the Central United States when it comes to politics, conservative. This probably stems from years of operating farms that offer only very thin profit margins.

Dale took the ranch we are on and turned it completely into a hunting paradise. He offers elk, bison, whitetail, fallow deer, and a few other exotic species. The genetics of the animals are very good and produce many large trophy-size specimens. The bison here are some of the best you can find. We finally got around to talking about bison and the hunting. I asked why I was the only one in the camp searching for the big wooly creatures. Dale chuckled and said the rest of the hunters had been on time, had filled their tags, and left. I guess I deserved that comment, and I knew he was only teasing me.

I then asked about numbers. Dale said there had been twenty-six hunters, and they all had taken respectable bulls, with ten being extremely large. I just looked at him and said, "YOU'VE GOT TO BE KIDDING." I asked in my best tone of voice, without sounding as if I were whining, if there were any bulls left for a fat farm boy like me. He said they had more hunters than normal, but Dale, in his refined way, tried to assure me that there were still some bison left on the ranch.

The best news I got was that Dale would be my guide. This would be great to have the ranch owner take me around as he would know the best areas to find my trophy. Yes, I said "trophy" as I was still optimistic that he could find a great bull for me. We ate a late lunch and headed out to see the ranch. It was very beautiful, and the fall colors added to the beauty. The terrain varied from rolling hills covered in grass to very deep, rugged canyons that were choked with oak and pine trees. I was surprised to learn that the bison spent a great deal of time in the canyons and trees. I always expected they would inhabit the grasslands full time.

We spent the afternoon driving around, talking farming, and looking at a few bison. We didn't see any good bulls, but I was encouraged to see there were still a few left. We returned to the ranch house at dark and enjoyed a wonderful meal and great camaraderie. My new friend from New York had taken a tremendous elk, scoring well over four hundred inches. That marked his fourth elk taken on the ranch, and he seemed to be OK with the tremendous amount of money he had spent. I really think he may have gotten rid of his elk fever, at least temporarily.

The next morning, we were out checking for buffalo when we

came across one of the many herds of fallow deer located on the ranch. They were in full rut, and the herd had two very good bucks traveling with the does. I had never experienced these deer in the wild and found them very beautiful. Out of nowhere, Dale asked if I wanted to take one of the bucks. I smiled and looked at him with that look of "What do you mean?" He said the one with the darker coat was extremely large for the species, and I really should have one for my trophy collection. What happened next will show you how easy it is to sell me on certain things. As Dale talked, the only words I had heard were "extremely large." Therefore, Dale, being a great salesperson, had me outside the truck and taking the dark fallow deer.

Now I know nothing about fallow deer, and I certainly don't know anything about their trophy size, but I now have one, and I am taking pictures. Next comes the news that I now owe $2,500 to Dale for the trophy fee. My left and right conscience is now talking to each other in silence, saying, "YOU'VE GOT TO BE KIDDING." They continue by letting me know how ridiculous it is to have taken this deer. It is not on my list of North American 29, and I did not intend to start a collection of introduced species to the Northern Hemisphere. My only thought is, *Why didn't you say something before I shot?*

All right, I can't hold Dale responsible for my actions, so I forgave him for being such a good salesperson, and we continued looking for bison. It's funny that he had waited until now to tell me he used to own some very large car dealerships in Western Canada and was a top seller. Go figure.

We came around a corner, up a little hill with the truck, and were looking back toward one of the very deep canyons. There was the single bison. It was headed out of the thickets and coming our way. A quick look through my binoculars confirmed what Dale had just told me, that it was a bull, and he looked to be very good. I asked what I should do, and Dale thought we should stay put and not move as movement might push him back to the canyon. I then asked about walking toward him, but Dale said, "The bison are used to the trucks on the farm but get very scared when they see people walking." Therefore, I sat and waited to see what the bull's intention was. He continued walking right to the truck as if he were on a mission. The closer he got, the better he looked. I inquired about the size, but Dale said only that he was a good bull. He was closing the distance fast, and we thought we should get outside to get ready for a shot.

Dale said, "Shoot very low and far forward as the bison's heart is very low and all the way to the front of the chest cavity." When the bull was within one hundred yards, I was instructed to "Take him." This now brings us back to the start of this chapter, with Dale telling me to shoot lower and farther forward. After reloading the second time, I fired the seventh shot at the big brute. I have never seen an animal with so much stamina. In my mind, I'm thinking how in the world did the Native American Indians get these "tanks" to the ground while using only the long bow? He had now taken seven shots from my .300 Weatherby Lazermark rifle. Finally, he crumbled in a pile. I was so embarrassed, but Dale could see my disappointment and assured me this scenario happens all the time.

As I got ready to take pictures, I was in awe at the size of this creature. We had no chance of repositioning him because of the size and were lucky he had gone down perfectly for great pictures. I now said a little prayer of thanks for the good fortune I had in finding a very good bull. At this point, I had no idea how good he was. After pictures, Dale had the help bring the loader tractor out and load the bison whole into the truck and return to the ranch. He weighed in at 2,600 pounds, making him over one and a quarter tons. His horns scored high enough to make him the thirtieth largest bison ever taken in the world. All I could say to myself was thanks for always being optimistic. The news of twenty-six bulls harvested didn't dampen my optimism. I used this information to inspire me to work harder.

I wanted to take the bison meat home with me as I had the pickup truck. I soon learned this would not be allowed as bison meat was under the same United States quarantine as beef coming across the border from Canada. Canada had been placed in this position by the discovery of "mad cow disease" in a herd of beef cattle.

Dale said I should be okay with the horns and the hide if the customs and immigration personnel at the border crossing knew the law regarding mad cow. I couldn't understand the difference that only taking the hide and the horns made, but I didn't question. I had a cousin working at a small port of entry in North Dakota, and I decided to use this as my point of crossing as I would at least have someone to help interpret the law if needed. The crossing went without incident, even though my cousin wasn't working when I crossed the border. I was now home and had my twenty-second species.

One and a quarter tons = 2500 pounds

CHAPTER 18

The Hunter's Favorite

I am soaked with perspiration, and I can't move. I can see the color of her eyes, even though it is barely daylight. She is very fit and toned and remains motionless. I wish I could get into a flatter position. She has me pinned down, and if I move, I may not have the chance I need to fulfill my dream. Now her sister appears, with the same thought on her mind. I can feel her breathing, and I notice she can't take her eyes off me. They look very alert, considering she and her sister have been up all night. Before I know it, I have more females looking at me with again the same thoughts on their minds. This is usually a good thing. There is hardly a man alive who wouldn't trade places with me at this moment.

No, this isn't a description of a ménage à trois but a very real predicament we can find ourselves in while elk hunting. My guide and I have just climbed to a very steep outcropping in an effort to get a vantage point for glassing at daybreak. As we reached the summit and popped over the top, there she was, standing only a few feet from me. I could see her and her sister. They were so close I could smell their breath. Upon a closer look, I realized we were in the middle of the whole herd of elk. A quick look around and I could see parts of two very nice bulls less than one hundred yards away. They were partially hidden in the timber. The only chance I had to take one of the bulls was to remain motionless and hope the cows didn't spook and take the bulls with them.

I have waited purposely until late in the book to write a chapter on wapiti, which is the Indian name for the North American elk. My fear was that you would be satisfied to read about elk and not pursue

184

the other chapters. Now it's your chance to say "YOU'VE GOT TO BE KIDDING!" Actually, my reasoning is the incredible love other hunters and I have for elk hunting. I wasn't very successful in my early elk hunts, so I wanted to have more of an upbeat tone in this book in the early chapters. The later years of my elk hunting produced some fantastic results.

I have "elk fever," and I'll bet if we took a poll that elk hunting would be the favorite big game hunt for hunters. If you ask about a hunt taking place near the hunter's home, whitetail would be the top in the poll, but here I am, talking about traveling out of town or out of state to hunt a big game species. Elk would be the number 1 choice. I can fully understand everyone's love of elk hunting as I have done more elk hunts than hunts for any other species.

Every hunter knows elk are majestic in the size of their body. They can grow unbelievably huge antlers, and hearing your first elk bugle is an incredible experience for a hunter. There is also something magical about their habitat. I have hunted elk in the rain forest, the darkest timber, the plains, the steepest mountains, and the pinion cedar country.

The first elk hunt I went on was in 1981 as four of us headed to White Sulfur Springs, Montana. My two brothers, Steve and Herb, and our good friend, Dan Wilson, accompanied me. These names you have seen numerous times in this book. The hunt to Montana was our first hunt together, and we tried to go together on as many as we could throughout the years. In 1981, I would say our hunting fund seemed to be quite full. We spent almost two weeks on the road and even included some mule deer hunting in the Dillon, Montana, country. We took some little deer, and Steve and Dan each got elk that were respectable. I think after this trip, we all decided that if we were going to hunt, we might as well leave the little ones to grow, and we should be trophy hunters.

It would be ten years after that hunt in Montana and nine elk hunts later that I found myself hunting the elk in this story. I was hunting around Steamboat Springs, Colorado, in October 1991. This is the hunt referred to in chapter 2 that produced the first species in my North American 29. Before I continue to write about this hunt, let me describe briefly the nine hunts leading up to 1991.

My brother Herb and I went twice for a week each time to the rain forest in the coastal mountains in Oregon. It was two years in a row, November 1983 and 1984. The rain was steady, and the elk were in hiding. We did see a few cows at times if there was a brief moment of sunshine. We never did see a bull. I went alone in the fall of 1985 to the breaks of the John Day River in Eastern Oregon. This was very beautiful country with great weather. I did see a Boone and Crockett mule deer but didn't have a tag. These three hunts were self-guided, and we were unsuccessful for elk.

Herb, Dan, Steve, and I made trips to Colorado and New Mexico in 1986, 1987, 1988, and 1989. In Colorado, we hunted in the Glenwood Springs area. In New Mexico, we hunted in the Chama area. Around Glenwood Springs is some of the steepest elk terrain I hunted as the creeks flowing from the White Mountains flattop region to the Colorado River drop in elevation very rapidly. These were all unguided hunts. In chapter 3, I wrote how Herb and I had passed on the huge mule deer to pursue the huge bull elk. We didn't get the bull or the deer on that hunt in 1986. We got a small four-by-four elk in 1986, and Herb got a nice five by six in 1987. We were unsuccessful on the other hunts.

The next trip we made to Colorado in 1990, we went on a supposed guided hunt. We responded to an ad in the back of one of the hunting magazines but didn't ask for references. It was a total disaster. Just a few of the problems included leaving camp in the morning after daylight and returning to camp before dark and very little land to hunt. We basically got a trail ride on the horses. I guess we should have known better than to go elk hunting with an outfitter whose name contained "Trail Riders." Dan, Herb, and I came home, again unsuccessful.

I am painting a rather bleak picture for a decade of elk hunting. I love elk hunting, and each time we went, we were just as optimistic as the previous hunt. Optimism can only carry you so far. Therefore, after the disastrous hunt last year in 1990, I vowed to change my strategy for determining where I would go to hunt elk. As you read in chapter 2, I had decided to use the services of a booking agent. I figured my time was worth something, and I couldn't keep going to places that tied up my time and produced zero results. I had no plans back then about taking the "North American 29," but I may have gotten started earlier if elk hunting had gone a little more favorably.

Don't get me wrong; you can still get involved with a hunt that is less than perfect and take some fine trophies. You just have a much better chance at success when using a booking agent because you can check references and have a mediator if indeed things go wrong.

Herb and I headed to Steamboat Springs, Colorado, in October 1991. Fred Romley of Sportsman's Adventures had lined up this hunt for us. The camp was very nice, and the outfitter's four-wheel-drive pickups were in pretty nice shape. The hunt was set up for us to hunt some private land surrounded by national forest and BLM land. We were very optimistic as usual. It really is hard not to be optimistic on elk hunts as one bugle or one fleeting look at a big bull can get your heart pumping. The procedure was to leave before daybreak every day and drive somewhere that we could climb to get some elevation before daylight. We were up at three thirty every morning to allow enough time to get where the elk might be. My brother and I thought this was great as we actually had an outfitter with a plan. When you self-guide like we had done so much of, it's hard to be this organized.

On day 2, I had the thrill of my life. We had gotten a look at a couple of very good bulls right at daylight. They were part of the elk herd my guide and I found ourselves in the middle of in the beginning of this chapter. We needed a small miracle to get a shot at the bulls. They were standing in the background, so we remained motionless as the cows had us pinned down. Any kind of movement would set off a bark from the cows and away the herd would go, with the bulls getting into the black timber immediately.

The elk rut in Colorado usually takes place in September. It was now the middle of October, and the two bulls were still bugling. I couldn't believe how vocal they were this morning. Their sparing began as a little tree scraping. Within minutes, they were butting heads, and then it turned into full-fledged fighting. They were so close the noise was deafening. The only trouble we had was the trees still mostly hid them. What we needed was for the two cows to actually run us over and the rest of the herd and the bulls to follow their lead and come our way. It usually doesn't happen that way in hunting, but I could hope. The bark from the cow startled me, but I knew that it couldn't be good news. The herd began a very quick retreat from our position. The bulls were gone first, but we remained motionless. I wanted to start yelling but realized quickly it wouldn't do any good. What happened next was so unexpected.

I thought back to all the elk hunts I had been on until now. Last year, I was hunting in Pagosa Springs, Colorado. I had gone on two elk hunts last fall. On one, we were hunting up near Wolf Creek Pass, and it was snowing very heavily. We had spent most of the day inside the timber as my guide said when it snows, the elk do a lot of moving around in the trees. We had seen quite a few elk, and toward the end of the day, we saw a cow walk through an opening about a hundred yards away. Before we had a chance to think, there were elk passing through the opening one by one. Fifty or more passed, and then the bulls were next. First a few spikes and then some rag horns, and then it hit me. I had better be ready when the big bulls show as they were sure to be last. Sure enough, a big bull showed, and I shot. There was absolutely no sign of any impact. The elk were all gone as quick as they had appeared in the dark timber. We ran to where the bull had been and scoured the snow for any sign of blood. None was found, and I was extremely disappointed. I don't know how I could have missed, but I did. I just chalked it up to buck fever.

Now as I got back to reality, the cows slowed down and stopped. The bulls apparently didn't like the idea of their harem running away, so they began to circle and gather them. My guide whispered that I should now get a chance for a shot as the cows would be worried what the bulls were doing. Sure enough, less than a few minutes later, the biggest bull was out in the open at about 125 yards. I wasted no time in getting into a sitting position. The shot was good, and I had my big bull. What an incredible change of events!

We approached the bull, and he is a fine six by six. He would be the start of my North American 29, but I didn't know this in 1991. I thanked God, and we chatted about how fast things could change when hunting. The picture taking was almost nonexistent as my camera didn't work. I got one or two photos with the guide's poor camera. I made a mental note to myself to buy the best camera I could afford to take on these hunts. The note must have worked as I have over two thousand pictures from the remaining hunts.

Upon returning to the camp, I learned from Herb that he had seen a bigger bull with a good-size herd. Evidently, they had crossed a fence before they were able to get a shot. The guide thought they had moved to a property that they couldn't hunt. As it turned out, the fence was just a cross fence and not a property boundary. Herb could have killed the big bull. In defense of the guide, it can be hard to keep track of properties when working in the wilderness. I ended with the biggest bull in the camp, but I was just so glad to get a nice six by six after so many years of trying. This bull, as mentioned earlier, is my number 1 of my North American 29.

The start of the "North American 29"

189

I never completely got rid of elk fever. In 1993, I traveled to Northern Michigan and took a fine Rocky Mountain elk. He scored 431 inches and went a long ways to reducing the fever. I didn't include him in my North American 29 as he is nonindigenous.

Again refer to Rule #1: Don't sit on the trophy!

CHAPTER 19

Santa Rosa

The Safari Club International convention has become an annual event. It is so special for me to attend as I can at times be somewhat of a recluse. For those of you who know me well, this statement may sound ridiculous, but I do have more of a shy nature. Attending the conventions forces me to be an active member of the world's hunting society. I would go to visit with past outfitters and hunters I've met. In reality, for the amount of time I spent hunting and being in camps with other hunters, I associated with a very small number of hunters. My love for farming occupied most of my time, so the people I meet in camps were not always remembered. I always felt terribly bad because at the camp, we would exchange business cards and promise to call one another, but it just didn't happen very often. The conventions served as a way for me to be reacquainted with the few hunters I had met in the past. I needed the atmosphere of outfitter exhibits and great numbers of attendees to push me toward my eventual goal. It was always interesting to use the convention to talk with people with similar goals as me. In my close circle of hunting friends, I was the only one trying to complete the North American 29, so the convention was special.

Over the years, a small number of hunters have become very close friends. It was one of these friends who gave me the idea to hunt on Santa Rosa Island. This piece of land off the coast of California is an island in the group known as the Channel Islands. My friend James had gone to Santa Rosa a few years back and taken a Roosevelt elk and a Rocky Mountain mule deer. The good reference he gave was more than enough for me to get excited about doing the same hunt.

As you read in the previous chapter, Roosevelt elk had been very elusive while hunting in the coastal mountains of Oregon, so the idea of a new place to try for one was very intriguing. I went ahead and booked the hunt with Gordon Long of Multiple Use Managers (MUM) for September 2005.

I flew into Santa Barbara, California, and took a short charter flight to the island of Santa Rosa. The camp was a very nice ranch house, full of optimistic elk and deer hunters. This group of hunters was by far the most diverse bunch I had ever met in a hunting camp. There was a doctor, a lawyer, a thoroughbred horse breeder, an owner of a logging company, a dentist, and me, the farmer. Gordon Long was there personally to run the camp and serve as a guide. What an organized hunter he turned out to be.

The canyons of Santa Rosa Island

Because of the private nature of the hunting the Long family brought to the island, we were allowed to hunt the same day we flew. We ate a late lunch and headed out to hunt with one guide for two hunters. Roosevelt elk and Rocky Mountain mule deer were transplanted to the island more than a hundred years earlier. They live on this beautiful island and easily reached trophy size for two reasons. First, the genetics are very good, and second, the Longs have done a tremendous job of protecting the resource. Overhunting is never allowed. The price for these hunts is quite expensive based on supply and demand, thus also helping to keep the quality of the animals very high. Thank God, I had filled my hunting fund last year in 2004 when Becky and I sold our farmland in South Dakota.

This set up the hunting fund on the full mark so I could finish the North American 29. I really had seller's remorse, but it did allow enough funds to complete my dream of taking all twenty-nine species in North America. The cost of this hunt approached $20,000, which would have been very hard to find before the land sale. As I think about it, it probably would have meant another new banker.

The 30" buck, score 201"

It was my partner's turn the first afternoon to take his trophy. He was hunting elk only, and I was on a combination hunt for both deer and elk. I was OK with not having the first chance as I knew good things happen to those who wait. We spent three or four hours looking in some deep canyons but didn't find any elk large enough. I was so glad to see that the hunt would not require massive amounts of hiking in and out of the large canyons as Gordon's idea of hunting was to glass and wait for our quarry to come to us. The evening meal was great as elk and deer were the main dishes.

Day 2 was sunny and beautiful. At daybreak, we spotted a very large mule deer in an oak-infested canyon. He was feeding in the bottom, keeping in the shadows caused by the mountain blocking the rising sun. The guide and I took off after him and, within a half hour, reached the point where he had actually bedded down. I did something unusual; I shot the deer in his bed. The shot turned out perfectly, and I had a great Rocky Mountain mule deer. We then hiked out with the horns and the hide and left the meat for the packers to bring out. I have never previously been on a hunt where the guide and I didn't have to bring the meat out first. This made it very easy for the overweight farmer who hadn't gotten in shape before the hunt started.

We spent the rest of the day looking for an elk for my partner but couldn't find anything to his liking. It was another good meal at the camp, coupled with some of the best visiting I've encountered. The hunters were full of energy because of the easy hunting conditions. Gone were the usual crossing of deep canyons and tall mountains. I got the usual teasing about the small deer I took. I was hoping it would be the best Rocky Mountain mule deer I had taken to date. Gordon said he would measure it in the morning and mumbled something about a trophy fee. I didn't pay much attention to his musings because I knew my contract said the fee started after a score of 200 inches.

Morning came, and the weather on the side of the island we were hunting was foggy. We sat on a small mountain and tried to glass up some elk. In between waves of fog, we did find a good bull. Since it was my turn again for a shot, Gordon and I took off in the fog in the general direction of the bull. We hadn't gone very far when the air cleared just enough for us to see the complete animal. He looked very good, and again, I did something I hadn't done before. The bull was looking straight at us, so I fired a shot right through the neck.

He dropped immediately, and I thought, YOU'VE GOT TO BE KIDDING. I've heard guys tell stories of how they made this shot, but I just never believed it was a viable option, so I had never tried it. I had my Roosevelt elk, and I thanked God again for my good fortune.

After we got pictures taken, we returned to the camp for lunch. Gordon and my hunting partner took off to find another bull elk. Everyone else in the camp had taken their animals. The pressure was on now for my partner as the charter plane would be back in the camp to pick us up around 4:30 p.m. His luck was good. He got his elk in about an hour and was back in time to pack and be ready for the plane. Gordon was busy measuring everyone's trophies. My partner got a beautiful elk that scored over 320. Mine was not very far behind with a nice 316. I was thrilled with that as it easily made the SCI record book. Next, Gordon scored my deer. I am quite good with numbers, and as the measuring progressed, I was mentally adding the score as it went. I knew the magic 200 inches was a real possibility. When the final score was done, it was 201, which produced a huge grin on Gordon's face. I'm thinking, seriously, one inch over the mark and now I owe the $1,500 trophy fee. I tried in vain to argue that we

Finally a Roosevelt Elk

should score the buck as a typical deer and then take the deductions, thus lowering the score below 200 inches. This argument failed just the same as my Stone sheep in chapter 4. Of course, I had to say to Gordon, "YOU'VE GOT TO BE KIDDING." I asked God that if I ever needed to pay a trophy fee again because I exceeded a certain size, at least let the score be substantially over the mark.

The following morning, I was checking in at the airport in Santa Barbara and had quite an experience. I had my horns with me, and they were exposed. I wanted to check them as baggage as I needed to get them to South Dakota so Burnie could do the taxidermy work. I was causing quite a scene because the ticket agent had never had a customer ask to check their elk antlers as baggage. I had the tips of the horns covered in rubber hose and tape, and the portion of the skull that was with the horns was covered, so it was a nice package. I made up my mind not to let my Irish temper flare, and after an hour, I finally convinced the agent that it was legal to ship horns. It is interesting to note here that I had checked many sets of horns onto airline flights in the past, but this would be the last time I needed to do this. The remaining hunts I had left didn't require me to check a large set of horns, which may have been a godsend. With the addition of the Roosevelt elk, I now have collected twenty-three species of my North American 29.

CHAPTER 20

Ground Shrinkage

I broke my promise. If you remember earlier in the book, I wrote of the need to use a booking agent to line up any hunt. I didn't follow my own advice in the story I'm about to tell you. This decision will prove to be a terrible mistake for me. Deer hunting is very exciting for most hunters. I have not been on an overly large number of deer hunts in my hunting career. It's not that I don't like deer hunting; it's just that the need to hunt the other species got in the way of the deer hunts.

Brother Steve and I walked around the Safari Club International (SCI) convention in Reno, Nevada, talking with many attendees, including past outfitters and old friends. It is January 2005, and we are among the approximately twenty thousand people attending this year's convention. If you have never attended this hunting show, you should also add this to your bucket list of things to see and do. Steve was researching a place to go hunt in Africa, and I was stumbling around, not looking for anything in particular. I only had five species left to finish the North American 29, one of which was the Columbia black-tailed deer. I only needed to book three hunts, though, as the polar bear scheduled for 2007 had been booked for three years already. I had paid $5,000 during the SCI convention in 2004. This money would hold a spot for me to hunt polar bears, but it would not protect the price. The cost of the tag and airline flights was now approaching $35,000 and had been increasing every year.

There are times when I act without thinking. I was about to do exactly that. The sheer number of outfitters displaying at the SCI is quite overwhelming for me. A great amount of discipline is required, at least on my part, not to leave this convention with the hunting fund very far in the negative. Over the years, my advice to friends who have joined me at the show for the first time has been "Leave all your credit cards and checkbook at home, and bring with you just enough cash to buy drinks and food during the stay." I should have listened to my own advice.

I met an outfitter who hunts for Columbia black-tailed deer around Medford, Oregon. I listened as he talked about the great bucks he had taken on previous hunts. His pictures were very impressive. I should have walked away without signing anything, but I didn't. I paid for half of a hunt scheduled for October 2005. I went against everything I have talked about in this book. I didn't use a booking agent, and I didn't check any references. As I said in a very early chapter, I am an easy sell, and I have to be careful not to buy things on impulse. I did not heed my own advice, so now I am going to hunt Columbia black-tailed deer in Oregon. If I am successful, this will give me the twenty-sixth species of my North American 29. The worst part of this story thus far is after I made the decision to pay for this hunt, I also convinced Steve he should do the same. We hadn't gone together on a hunt for any kind of deer since the late '90s when we were together in Mexico for desert mule deer. On that hunt, I didn't get a deer, and he ended with a very small one. With this lack of success, I was surprised he chose to go with me to Oregon.

Over a couple of cold beers that evening, we actually felt pretty excited that we were going to Oregon to hunt. We kept thinking how fortunate we were last fall when we took those two huge black bears. We truly thought we were on a roll and our optimism was all that we would need to be successful in taking a blacktail. Every hunter needs this kind of optimism, and I think, as I stated in earlier chapters, that hunters are the most optimistic lot. Steve and I have lived our lives exactly this way.

The flight to Medford, Oregon, was uneventful until we landed and met our outfitter at the airport. As we gathered bags, we got our first YOU'VE GOT TO BE KIDDING. He informs us that instead of a camp in the hunting area, we are going to stay in Medford at a motel. This may or may not be detrimental to our success, but we just wish we had known before leaving home as we could have left many things home, like our bulky sleeping bags. Steve and I talk and say we won't let this change our optimism.

We are to meet early for breakfast in the morning. The plan is for all three of us to hunt together for the day. We arrive after daylight in an area we can hunt. There is actually a lone buck out on a very high steep mountainside, and he looks very good. Steve says go ahead and try for him, so the guide and I head up the very steep mountain. We are only a short distance up the mountain, and we learn later the deer went into the timber almost immediately. Steve had watched our stalk from the seat of the truck but had no way to communicate to us that the buck was gone. The rest of the day we stayed on the same mountain, thinking we might see the buck again, but no luck. This would be our only sighting of this buck, even though I hunted every day in this same spot.

The lonely hillside that was the total area I could hunt!

That evening at supper, we mention to our guide/outfitter that our hunt was booked as a one-guide, one-hunter scenario. Thus far, it has been two hunters and one guide. The outfitter tells us that it's hard to get someone to guide us, but he does have someone the day after next. We humor him and say OK but think how bad this is starting to get. On the morning of the third day, we are back to the mountain we have hunted the first and second days. Actually, it is more like a steep hill, and we can hunt only one small area on one face of this hill. We suddenly realize we have no territory to hunt other than this hill and the logging roads in the area.

This morning of the third day, my guide has to go somewhere, so he leaves me alone on the side of the hill for most of the day. Steve actually has his own guide today, and they drive around all day in an area with many logging roads. It appeared that they didn't have permission to hunt the areas they were driving through.

He's not bad considering the conditions

I won't go into all the details that make this hunt the worst I have ever taken part in. The hunt was not worth the money we had paid for it; in fact, if we had paid zero, it still would qualify as the worst. I felt especially bad because I had convinced Steve to join me on this fiasco.

The evening of the third day, the guide Steve had for a grand total of one day quits. All I could think is *God, this sounds familiar,* and I said to Steve, "YOU'VE GOT TO BE KIDDING." This scenario of the guide quitting marks the third time in just the last ten years. José quit while I was hunting Coues deer, and our young native quit while Kiel and I were finishing our Caribou hunt in the Northwest Territories. Steve was upset with me, as well he should have been, as I was the reason his guide quit. I had let my Irish temper flare when Steve told me all they did was drive around the country. To me, it appeared our outfitter was trying to appease Steve by giving him the tour of the area. I told the young guide the entire scenario was ridiculous, and he left.

I will stop wasting words to describe this hunt. It went from already terrible to much worse. I did take a Columbia black-tailed deer, thanks to my self-guiding abilities. He scored high enough to make the SCI record book; therefore, I met my goal of taking a better-than-average representative of the species. Steve hunted hard but was unable to connect with any trophy on this hunt. We returned home very disappointed. We stayed upbeat and moved on to our other hunts with true optimism. I now had my twenty-fifth species of the North American 29.

CHAPTER 21

Tree Hugger

I don't hide the fact that I am a conservative and also a registered Republican, although I'm not sure anymore if the words "conservative" and "Republican" can be used together. It is interesting that I would call this chapter tree hugger. The hunt in the last chapter for Columbia black-tailed deer took place in Oregon, which gets a rap for having a few people who some might call tree huggers. This chapter has nothing to do with politics, so I won't go any further in depth there. It does have to do with the only North American species of big game animal that is, at times, a true "tree hugger." If you haven't guessed it, I am talking about a mountain lion. They can and do spend some time in trees, and most of the ones hunters take each year are the result of the lions being treed by good hunting dogs. Thus, the term "tree hugger" fits them. Lions also take much of their prey from the perfect hiding place provided by trees and branches.

Marvin James of James Guide Service was highly recommended by my good friend John Gates. Marvin headquarters in Flagstaff, Arizona. He is one of the best outfitters using dogs to hunt lions. What makes Marvin even better than most outfitters using dogs is the fact that his dogs can hunt lions on dry ground. The majority of outfitters, especially in the northern areas of North America, use dogs that only can track lions on snow. This greatly limits the amount of time during the year they can actually hunt. Marvin can go hunt at any time. We are here in December, but there is no snow in the Flagstaff area.

My brother Steve flew into Phoenix from North Dakota, and after overnighting at our home in Gilbert, Arizona, we drove together to

Marvin's house and camp outside Flagstaff. On the way, we went by the Game and Fish and bought our licenses over the counter. You can buy a tag per day for lions. It's too bad we couldn't get other licenses as easily as lion. It's especially hard to draw an Arizona tag for any species when you apply as a nonresident. Their system does keep the quality of the animals very high.

A day in camp relaxing is always welcome, and we did just that the day we arrived. The following day, we set out to walk and climb a few small mountains in a crisscross pattern, looking for sign or tracks. We checked a few places where the lions had marked their territory, but all we found were old signs. The forecast is for snow, so Marvin decided we would wait for a light dusting and then go out and look for fresh tracks. In the camp, I had time to look back on previous hunts. I was suddenly having some of the feelings I experienced last year in Oregon.

Hunting is wearing on me. You may find that statement hard to believe, but I'm quite tired of the pressure I've placed on myself to finish the twenty-nine. You're probably thinking, YOU'VE GOT TO BE KIDDING. You may be asking, "How in the world would anyone get tired of hunting?" Well, I have, and I'm quite disappointed in myself for these feelings. Last fall, I experienced a bit of depression as I was hunting black-tailed deer. It was not just one factor causing me anguish but a combination of the time I've been away from home in the past fifteen years, the huge amount of money I've spent to get to this stage, and the yo-yo dieting I've done trying to stay in some kind of reasonable shape.

I also notice I've had less patience with my guides and outfitters than in the earlier hunts. There are days when I don't want to glass another mountainside or traverse through that huge canyon in front of me or even get out of my sleeping bag in the morning. I have found the need to tell myself all the time, "Buck up and get going as any hunter would love to be in your position."

Snow started falling around 6:00 p.m. Marvin has a contact north and west of Flagstaff toward the Grand Canyon. The report from him is fairly heavy snow in the hunt area. Our luck couldn't be any better as mountain lions move mostly under the cover of darkness. Our plan is to travel the back roads all night searching for fresh tracks in the new snow. Our only curse would be an extreme amount of snow making the roads impassable. Doug Star hunts with Marvin and has his own dogs. We will split up and look in two different places for the tracks. During the all-nighter, it was amazing to see how many tracks the deer, elk, and mountain lions produced in just a few hours. I had no idea there would be that much movement. We found some lion tracks and actually spent a large amount of time analyzing the ones that were single. Marvin said it's futile to follow any multiple tracks as the big males always travel alone.

The plan to check two areas has worked perfectly. A single track has been found closer to Flagstaff. Steve is excited as he will have first chance to take his trophy. We spend a great deal of the morning hours researching exactly where the lion is heading and which roads he has crossed and not crossed. These guys really have a plan in mind all the time. They don't release the dogs until they are sure they are in the general area the lion can be found. The dogs are released, and the chase is on. The lion is headed generally where Marvin and Doug thought, and it takes only a few miles for the dogs to do their job and get the mountain lion treed. Steve has his trophy.

Sometime around three o'clock the following morning, we find another single big fresh track. Marvin says, "This will be my lion." Now that's optimism. I can't wait to see the dogs in action. Marvin says we will let them out at around eight o'clock as we can't check the roads because there are none except the one we are on. The pickup seat provides a place for some sleep as we wait for first light.

As I lay back, my mind wonders to a favorite hunting memory. My brother Herb and I are hunting Roosevelt elk in the rainy costal ranges in Oregon. We are west of Portland and have put a few days of hunting behind us. These days have been filled with lots of mountain climbing, and we covered many miles. We had been getting started by daybreak every morning and staying out after dark. In a word, we were exhausted. We had made some friends of the local elk hunters while visiting the local pub in the evening when we ate supper. They told us a good spot to try for elk, so we decided we would check it out. We left our motel about 2:00 a.m. and arrived at the "hot spot" about 3:30 a.m. Daylight hits about 6:00 a.m., so we put the pickup seats back and proceeded to nap until we had enough daylight to hunt. Well, we slept just a little too long, and when we awoke, it was about 6:45 a.m. We got out of the truck, and what we saw made us look at each other and say, "YOU'VE GOT TO BE KIDDING." All around the pickup truck in the nice, soft, wet ground were dozens of elk tracks. The whole herd of at least fifty animals had passed right by us while we slept. There were literally tracks on both sides of the truck. How exciting that could have been!

Another memory that came to mind happened in Colorado while elk hunting with my good friend Dan and brother Herb. We were guiding ourselves and had gone our separate ways during the day. When met at the camp that night, I must have looked really sick as they both commented that I looked like crap. Thanks a lot, guys. I had just experienced what happens when a hunter does what he is told not to do. I had been in some very good elk habitat most of the day. It was heavily timbered, and I literally could smell elk as I walked. Sometime during the afternoon, I needed a bathroom break. I joked with myself as I raised my hand and said, "Teacher, I have to go number 2." I was on a rather steep part of the mountain, and I stood my rifle against a tree and proceeded to lower my britches and do my duty.

At that exact moment, a huge six-by-six elk appeared less than fifty yards from me. He was not looking at me, so I was immediately on the ground crawling on my hands and knees to get to my rifle about ten feet away. I must have been quite a sight, and I think the elk stayed around just long enough to laugh at some crazy hunter with his pants down on the ground trying to get to his gun. I didn't have a chance as he was gone when I reached the rifle. How many times have I heard "Keep your rifle with you at all times"? The bull I saw was the very best I had seen in my hunting career. I just could have cried, and I must have looked awful when I got back to the camp. The boys didn't let me live that incident down.

I awaken to the bark of the dogs as they apparently know when they are about to be let loose to go to work. Marvin and Doug have picked out a few dogs to use on the fresh lion track. I was so thrilled to see how quickly the dogs got the scent of the lion and took off on the track. Our plan was that Doug would try to stay close to the dogs and Marvin and I would trail behind, traveling as fast as I could go. The lion must have known the dogs were getting close as he went up and down the steepest canyons. The lion was headed almost due north, and then I got the bad news. Marvin said if we didn't get him treed in the next five miles, he would end up reaching the boundary of the Grand Canyon National Park. Once he was inside the park, we would not be allowed to hunt him anymore. I picked up my pace immediately after hearing that news. I was hoping I wouldn't be the cause of not getting this lion.

Marvin assures me that, looking at the size of the track, this is a good lion. I agreed with him as the track looks very large. I was a bit apprehensive when I booked a mountain lion hunt in Arizona as this state is not known for bigger lions. Typically, the northern areas of the United States and southern areas of Canada produce bigger trophy animals. However, the size of this track makes me believe I have made a great decision to hunt in Arizona.

The day is very warm with the temperature close to 60 degrees. The little snow we got overnight will be gone in the afternoon. After a few hours on the lion trail, the pace of travel has slowed as the dogs seem to have a hard time staying on the scent. The ground now is about half snow-covered and half open. Marvin says we would be better off now if the snow had all melted and the lion was running on dry ground as the dogs would be all over him. That eased my mind as I didn't know if we could find him if all the snow melted.

After lunch, with the snow being mostly gone, the dogs are on a terror pace. We can barely hear them anymore as they are a long way in front of us. The lion is finding the steepest, roughest country to take us through as he attempts to lose his pursuers. The dogs are relentless as is Doug. He has been with them the entire time. It takes very good conditioning to walk and keep up to the dogs. Once again, I have failed to take seriously the training I should have done before the hunt. When will I learn?

It is now after 3:00 p.m., and we can hear the dogs again, although they sound extremely far away. We have been following now for over seven hours. Marvin informs me that the dogs have treed the lion. I want to ask how he knows this, but I hold my tongue and think there must be something in their barking that changes when their work is complete. We quicken the pace. The lion may not stay put although most times, they are done running. An interesting note here is if the dogs ever get the lion to run instead of walk, the hunt is all but over. The lions can only run all out for a quarter of a mile, and then they are so tired the dogs catch them easily. Down we go through another canyon, and when we get to the top on the other side, the dogs have become very loud. Marvin says they are just ahead.

Tired out old Tom

207

The picture of my trophy lion in the tree is wonderful. He is panting heavily, and the dogs are so noisy it's hard to talk. I take a picture of him lying on a big branch of the tree. I ask Marvin how to make the best shot, and he explains to shoot through the front shoulder. I thought this would be the best choice, but I asked anyway. I didn't want to go through another seven-hour hike. One shot from the .300 Weatherby and the mountain lion loses his grip on the tree branch and lands on the ground. The dogs are all over him. Marvin says it's good to let the dogs maul the big cat a little so they get a sense of accomplishment. I am scared they will do damage to the hide, but Marvin says it will be all right. I'm thinking, *Let's get this procedure stopped quickly,* and he calls off the dogs. I have a beautiful lion.

He's so cute

We take care of the skinning and head out for the trucks. We are not as far from a road as I thought, and we are back in about two hours, well before dark. The Grand Canyon Park boundary is only a half mile from the tree where the lion ended his run. That is cutting it pretty close. I haven't had time to say my prayer of thanks, so I do it on the way back to the trucks. I am thankful as I now have twenty-six of the North American 29.

Actually, completing my goal is becoming more real all the time. Later this year, I have a grizzly bear hunt in British Columbia; a woodland caribou hunt planned for Newfoundland, Canada; and then the following spring for the polar bear. I have quite a journey behind me but a very big challenge yet to come.

Steve and my lion

CHAPTER 22

Humpbacks

Part 1

I'm waiting patiently for the call. Nothing happens again today. It's already June 15, 2006, and I am still working on the farm, finishing planting soybeans. I should have finished two weeks earlier, but the planting season has been delayed by a cold, wet spring. The hunt I had planned for this spring should have happened already, but I haven't even left South Dakota to begin it. Each day, I wait for the call from Gary Drinkall from Chetwynd, British Columbia, to advise me of the status of the grizzly bear emergence from their winter dens.

Gary has graciously offered to call me when the bears are being seen. This will allow me to use the two weeks I have booked with him to actually hunt them instead of waiting for them to emerge from their sleep. As each day passes, it seems odd that the bears have not appeared. I always thought they came out in early to mid-May. I guess they are on a different timetable this year. Possibly the same weather pattern causing our late planting season is responsible for the bear's emergence.

I wait for the start of this hunt, and my thoughts go back to the three different hunts needed to take my Alaskan brown bear. In addition, the memory of the three hunts for black bear causes some concern. Bears have been my nemesis thus far, but I'm hoping to change that with this hunt. It's not starting as planned, but I am optimistic that will change. Gary is a good outfitter, and when the bears do emerge, he will have a plan to provide a great hunt.

The call comes late in the evening. The bears are out. Gary says they have seen a few. He also comments, "The weather is unusually warm but not to worry as the hair on the bears still looks very good." I hadn't even thought about the hair until he brought it up, but now the worry sets in. I think, YOU'VE GOT TO BE KIDDING. I know the later the season runs and the warmer the temperatures, the greater the chance the bears will be rubbed. The bears actually rub the hair off their bodies when the temperatures get too warm. In the den during the winter, their hair continues to grow to keep them warm while they sleep, so when they emerge in the spring, they have a luxurious coat. This is why hunters like to take spring bears. I will need a little Almighty intervention to keep the hair on for another two weeks.

I have been packed for a month, so I load the gear in the truck, and away I go. I am driving again to Canada just as I did for the bison hunt. As I said, I like to drive. This trip will be twenty-five hours, and I will drive it straight through so I don't miss any days hunting. The trip is filled with extra excitement as I am able to see the freshly emerging crops on all the farms from South Dakota to British Columbia.

Arrival at the camp brings a sigh of relief. Gary and Monique, along with his parents, operate a large cattle operation, and they produce the grains they feed their livestock on the farm, so we have much in common. The facilities to accommodate me for the hunt were ideal. I met Blaine, who is Gary's partner; he also farms, so how could it get any better? The only problem I faced with the guys was the politics involved between our two countries concerning mad cow disease. The Canadian cattle industry depends heavily on their ability to ship cattle to beef packers in the United States. The border was currently closed to their cattle because mad cow disease was found in a herd of cattle in Canada. The United States doesn't have mad cow, and we don't want to get it, thus the quarantine. Gary and Blaine didn't like it when I told them they should develop markets for their cattle besides the United States. I think they had already thought of that, but they haven't had the support of the Canadian government.

As that conversation had gone so poorly, I sure wasn't going to bring up the fact that the United States has also become a dumping ground for much of their wheat.

Aside from our political quarreling, the Drinkalls couldn't be nicer people, and their hunting operation is first class. The equipment is perfectly maintained and renewed often. It's always refreshing to see outfitters who care enough of their clients to see that equipment is replaced.

I am here for a fourteen-day hunt for common grizzly bear, and I was prepared to spend the time necessary to get my bear. Nothing changed here; I am a driven person as you've probably gathered by now. If it takes all fourteen days, it will still be far less than the thirty-seven days I found necessary to take an Alaskan brown bear. The strategy for the hunt to begin with is to visit sites where some of the cattle have succumbed to Mother Nature. The bears find these cattle and visit the sites at least every other day. We would be checking at various times to see if feeding is occurring. If this plan doesn't work, we are going to pack up and head for the taller mountains and set up camp to use spot and stalk techniques. This is the same way we hunted the black bears on Queen Charlotte Islands and for brown bear on the Alaskan Peninsula.

The first few days we do exactly what the plan called for. We check the dead cattle for signs of feeding. At one site, there is some bear activity, so we go early in the morning before daybreak and wait most of the day to see if a bear shows up for lunch. When nothing happens for a couple of days, we look at other sites. We are also driving on a few logging roads, checking the low mountains for the bears to be out eating grass. This year, the grass is even slow starting. The rut should also be occurring, so we should see some activity related to that. I haven't seen a bear in the first six days, so I have no idea if the rut is happening or not.

Day number 6 produces a look at a bear, but after a relatively short stalk, we determine the bear is much too small. It is beautiful, though, with a full coat of hair, and this makes my day. The worry about hair loss is deferred for now. I wouldn't be so concerned about the hair except that my brown bear had all his hair gone by the time I got him. It appeared that rodents had eaten it down to his baby hair while he was sleeping in the den. The fact that it was almost dark when I took him didn't allow checking the hair until he was on the ground. I was disappointed in the hair, but I would not have passed on him anyway. I was so thrilled to get him. The hope is on this hunt that if a bear is taken, he will not be bald.

After day 7, Gary decides we better pack up, leave the flatlands, and begin the pack trip to the bigger mountains. It will take us all day to get where we will make camp, so we get going early. We actually make good time, have time to hunt, and find a small bear right at dark. This is very encouraging, and I sleep well this night. The next morning, we run across a bear crossing the road at daybreak. He looks good, so we start a long walk through some of the beautiful countryside, but we never get another look at him.

Later that evening, we see two bears a long way off, but it gets dark before we can get a closer look. The next morning, we look, but they escape our view. We then cover many miles and view the gorgeous scenery. There are many roads, and we drive as many as we can to see if we can spot any bears. The next day, we have a cloudy day with a few sprinkles, so we anticipate the bears are not moving.

The next day is sunny, and we are expecting something exciting. We have become a little ragged. Ten days of rising at 3:30 a.m. and retiring at 11:30 p.m. has made for some pretty tired people, and we are starting to get on one another's nerves. This is typical of long hunts. The pressure the outfitter is under to produce a trophy animal for the hunter and the pressure the hunter places on himself to take a trophy animal can cause a banging of heads after a time. We needed something to take our focus away from our task.

We got exactly that when we heard the Yamaha ATV come down the road. It was a local Native American, and he had successfully taken a small bear a short distance from our camp. He was a nice guy and told us he spends most of his time hunting. When he left, I could see Gary wasn't very happy. I asked what was going on, and he told me, "The natives such as the guy we just met are able to hunt and fish all year round without a license. They can take as many animals as they want, and they take plenty. It hurts the chances for the animals to get to trophy size." I'm thinking, YOU'VE GOT TO BE KIDDING. It seems ridiculous to think someone can hunt and fish all year without a tag when it is so hard to draw a tag in most parts of North America, not to mention the high costs sport hunters pay. I'm paying $12,500 plus a $2,000 trophy fee if I get a bear, and he does it for nothing. I guess I shouldn't complain as I still am fortunate to have a chance to get a bear. If I sound like I'm whining, I am. I always forget all the injustice we have done to the Native Americans and that they should have more free things given to them. I am joking here and really don't want to use this forum for any political agenda.

We awaken at 4:00 a.m., which is a little later than we have been getting up. We head immediately down the road and haven't gone over two miles when we see two bears high up on the mountain. We spend an hour looking at them with the binoculars. They appear to be a boar and a sow engaged in the rut. The mountainside is very steep, and Blaine is devising a plan to go after them. Gary has set up a video camera on a tripod to film us for his camp advertising. This is causing some friction with Blaine, who thinks it's time to go after the bears before they disappear into the trees. Gary is doing a live interview with me about how we are going to get to the bears. I understand the need for what Gary is doing; I just question the timing. Then again, you know my theory about how the guide is always right. This will be no exception as the bears will either be there or not.

Two hours pass before we decide to hike up the steep old grade to get a closer look at the pair of bears who are out feeding. It is steeper than it appears from the bottom as they all are. We are making little progress, and after two hours, we are only halfway to the bears. For whatever reason, they now run for the timber. Possibly, they caught a whiff of our scent as the wind is blowing up the mountain. Blaine decides we should continue to climb to the top where the bears disappeared, wait, and see if they return. It's a far stretch, but it could happen. Two more hours and we have made it to the area where we are going to wait.

As we sit on the mountain, we suddenly realize the temperature is getting quite warm. At 1:00 p.m., it's 90 degrees. We prepared for this, but we didn't bring enough water. Although very uncomfortable, we have to stick it out as we have a very good vantage point to glass the surrounding mountainsides. We can't see any bears, but we do pick up a few mountain goats. The hours pass, and then the unexpected happened at about 4:00 p.m. At the bottom of the mountain where we were originally parked this morning, there is something moving down the road. We can't see exactly what the brown spots are until they get into the full sunlight. All I can say is "YOU'VE GOT TO BE KIDDING.

The bear mountain I scaled and then rolled down to get to my "hump back"

There, on the road, are the two bears we are looking for. Wow, they are exactly where we were filming this morning! Blaine looks at me and says we need to make a decision—take a dangerous fast trip down the mountain or wait and see if they might start back up. The decision is made quickly, and we start the steep trek down to the road.

Blaine thinks we can make it in an hour and hopes the bears will still be somewhere we can see them. God, this is true déjà vu as I am tripping and falling just like the trip off the mountain to get the brown bear. It's the same as that, with slippery rocks on very steep terrain. We take time every few minutes to check the position of our prey. So far, so good. We continue to get lower, I fall, and my rifle takes a hit against a rock. Why is it I'm always going downhill too fast? A quick check looking through the scope shows everything to be OK. I am relieved after the incident in Alaska when the scope was fogged. We continue down, but we haven't seen our quarry for fifteen minutes. Suddenly, they appear slightly above us, but they are moving down. We wait to see what will happen next.

"Boo Boo"

They move into the trees and out of sight again. The next time they appear, they are down on the road again. We are now close enough to continue all the way down, and we do so. On the bottom, we head for the road, and sure enough, they are there. The distance is about two hundred yards, and when they clear some timber alongside the road, I decide to take the shot. I am using a little tree branch for my rest, and it works perfectly. One shot and the bear spins around as if he were hit too far back. Now we have a wounded bear, and I'm unhappy. I tell Blaine the shot I made was good, but I don't know about the rifle or the scope. I tell him I am going to shoot again. If I miss, I want him to use his rifle and back me up. I shoot, and Blaine shoots shortly after me. The bear is still moving, so we shoot again. This time he is down, and I exhale a sigh of relief.

I've seen bigger bears, but this one is mine, and I couldn't be more thrilled. I thank God and praise Blaine for making the right call. We then proceed to get some pictures. He is a healthy bear with the most beautiful coat of silver-tipped hair. The hair is intact, and he will make a great life-size mount. His claws are long and curved like those of very big bears, so I know he is an older, mature animal.

Gary is not happy with us when he sees the bear. It is much smaller than he was expecting and gives us grief about shooting Boo-Boo, Yogi Bear's sidekick. As we analyze, we think the two bears were a female and a grown cub instead of a boar with a female in heat. Anyway, we can't change the size now. I am completely satisfied to have taken a species of bear in just twelve days of hunting instead of three hunts. This bear gives me my twenty-seventh species in my quest.

Part 2

After returning home from Chetwynd, British Columbia, at the end of June, it was time to catch up on the farming. Irrigation season had started, and it is a full-time job keeping center pivots running. The summer was pretty normal, if there is such a thing in the modern world. Rainfall in South Dakota is usually on the short side in the months of July and August, so we use irrigation to supplement our corn and bean crops.

During the remaining summer months, I had the time to try another grizzly bear hunt. The bear I took at Chetwynd didn't make the minimum score for entry into the SCI record book. This went against the goal I had that all the animals in my collection of the North American 29 had to meet the minimum score or higher. A few people told me that the biggest grizzly bears come from areas where their diets consisted of some salmon but the area they lived in was outside the boundary that would classify them as Alaskan brown bear. The search was on to find an outfitter to fulfill my need. It turned out Cabela's Outdoor Adventures had just the outfitter I needed to have an opportunity to take another grizzly.

Hoping I would take a bear with skull measurements big enough to reach into the SCI records, I booked with Bob Adams from Aniak, Alaska. Excitement always precedes a hunt, but this time, I wasn't as excited as normal. I had become completely burned out on hunting and wasn't looking to hunt in any more cold weather.

Bob has been in the outfitting business in Alaska for a long time. Immediately after meeting him, I knew this would be a good hunt. The condition of his airplanes was perfect. He reminded me of Art and Crystal Thompson's attention to detail. If you remember, they were our outfitter when Becky and I went on the couple's retreat to British Columbia in the year 2000. Bob was a little blunt, or should I say quite to the point during conversation, but I like someone who tells it like it is. He reminded me when we got to the base camp that success on big grizzlies could not be guaranteed. I knew that little fact, but I'm glad he tells the clients. Maybe it's a well-thought-out ploy to make sure his hunters are giving 100 percent effort when out in the spike camps.

The flight from Aniak to the base camp was quite unique because of the terrain. First, you start out crossing a very marshy area that looks like the Mississippi River Delta, and then it is small rolling hills before getting to the edge of the bear mountains. The base camp was very functional and conservative as many of Alaskan outfits are. The state of Alaska doesn't protect the outfitters' territories as they do in Canada. Hence, I think the outfitters in Alaska have a hard time justifying a large expense in base camps when someone new may move in right across the river or somewhere close by.

The fight to the spike camp was more spectacular than the ride to the base camp. This part of Alaska has very few trees, even in the lower elevations, so the mountains looked very gray with no vegetation toward the peaks. I thought this might be a reason for success as there would be fewer hiding places for our quarry. As I would later learn, this idea would be another of my theories that would be just that, a theory. The camp consisted of two tents, and I thought that a bit odd out here in the wilderness. Soon, I learned the second tent was to accommodate another guide, thus giving me two people to help me get my grizzly. Normally, one guide is provided, but I have two.

I haven't asked, but I am assuming "Old Humpie" is very far away. Yes, I'm told, the bear is very far away, but we are going to try to get a closer look. I survey the landscape, and it looks like a relatively flat three miles of terrain between us and our quarry. In the middle is what appears to be a small stream. We grab our gear and head out at a very fast pace. Hiking in much of the Alaskan terrain is never easy. The tundra holds countless surprises, and every other step usually means a slip into the little water pockets lying on the tundra.

Our first surprise comes after an hour of hiking. The small stream is actually a very large river. We couldn't tell at first look as the river

Grizzly country of Western Alaska

is situated in a very deep canyon. It becomes a daunting task to cross the river and canyon. It takes us an entire hour. After reaching the other side, a look at the area where our bear should be produces a mountainside devoid of creatures. Big bears are typically on the move, and this one was no exception. After conversing with my guides, it was the consensus to continue to the bear's last known location and see if we could find him in the open somewhere. We walked very fast, yet the remainder of the trip clocked in at two hours. It's no wonder he looked so small as we looked from the camp. A total of four hours of hiking took us to get to the area we first spotted the bear. As usual, the country is so much bigger than it appears. We never saw him again.

We spent the next few hours glassing the mountains on our side of the miniature canyon. I wasn't looking forward to the return trip to the camp, but we had to make it. The river crossing didn't go well as we couldn't find the shallower area we used on the trip out. We ended up with water over our hip boots and wet from the waist down. I was glad to get back to the tent and was exhausted from the daylong hike. The guides had worked hard, so supper was very quick, and everyone went right to bed. The next three days we spent walking into new areas and glassing. We saw a few bears but nothing that excited us enough to actually stalk them.

The weather remained very respectable with nice warm temperatures during the day. My guides told me it would be hard to find bears with the sunny weather we have had for the past week. This is a direct contradiction to the thinking of the guides on my brown bear hunts. A warm, sunny day would produce better results. Again, the guide is always right. This morning was cold, and we hiked around the end of the mountain and glassed some new country. I was terribly cold just sitting, so I did what any cold hunter would do. I tried to run up the mountain. The run lasted all of five minutes, and I was exhausted, but I was warm. I just couldn't handle the cold anymore. The rest of the morning, we glassed the valleys and mountains in our immediate sight. We saw a sow and two cubs a great distance away. Around noon, we headed back to the camp for my favorite lunch of bologna sandwiches.

As the guides were preparing lunch inside the mess tent, I was busy glassing the mountain behind the camp. I did a double take when I saw it in my binoculars. I caught it just as it crossed over the top to our side of the mountain. I yelled out, "YOU'VE GOT TO BE KIDDING!" and this brought the guides running from the tent. I pointed at the mountainside and said, "All the walking and looking we've done and here is a bear spotted right near the camp." Just a few minutes later, we were heading up the mountain to intercept the intruder. Why is it that every mountain is much more formidable

A great "hump back"

than they appear to be? Our plan was to climb quickly from the camp to the area the bear was feeding on berries. As noted earlier, the bear would be on the move, so it was critical that we got up this mountain. Just because it looked as if he was heading down the mountain, we had to be realistic and think any direction was a possibility.

Occasionally, the pendulum of luck swings to the hunter's advantage. As we are climbing, we try to hide and then carefully check on the position of the bear. Our pace is more than I can maintain, but I'm not quitting. Suddenly, I

221

get the break I need as the bear decides to take a nap on the open mountainside. This is great as we now quickly close the gap. Our timing is good as we reach the level on the mountain where the bear is located. I connect on the first shot, the bear falls to the right, and down the mountain it rolls. The scene is identical to my Rocky Mountain bighorn rolling down the shale-covered wash in Alberta. I can't believe how far the bear is traveling. It appears as though I won't need another shot, but I don't know as the mountain is so steep; he just keeps going. He covers half the distance it took us one hour to climb in just minutes. He comes to a halt around a huge boulder in the middle of a streambed.

The hunt is over, and I have an Alaskan common grizzly bear. He is a real beauty with a gorgeous coat. I make some quiet time to thank God for my good fortune and then begin to take pictures. He easily meets the SCI minimum score. I especially am thankful for the fact that I have hunted the humpback bear twice and have taken two beautiful bears. Once again, with the common grizzly bear, I have twenty-seven species.

Bob flies in to pick me up.

CHAPTER 23

"Newfies"

I am a fun-loving person. Work hard and play hard certainly fits my personality. Having now collected twenty-seven species of my North American 29, I have experienced a wide range of styles of hunting camps. I have had some of the best outfitters in the world. A few stood out as very task-oriented and were a little more serious. A few were the exact opposite, spent less time on the details and strived for just the final result. Some hunts are just more fun than others are, which is not a criticism of any of my outfitters' style. With the exception of a few, I enjoyed them all, and they have done a wonderful job for me.

It is October 2006, and I am going again to Canada to hunt a woodland caribou. I haven't been to Eastern Canada since 9/11 when we went to Quebec in search of Quebec-Labrador caribou. The outfitter is Mt. Peyton Outfitters out of Gander, Newfoundland, Canada. My flight in from Montreal lands safely in Gander. I have been to the Gander airport one other time. Becky and I earned a free trip by selling sunflower seed to other farmers in 1979. The trip was a week in Costal Del Sol in Spain, and our plane from Fargo, North Dakota, stopped to refuel in Gander before crossing the Atlantic. I remember looking out the airplane window as we sat on the ground. The wind was blowing snow, and it just looked very inhospitable. At that time, I made a mental note that I didn't want to visit here again. Twenty-seven years later, I am back.

A very nice gentleman who works for Don Tremblent, the owner of Mt. Peyton, meets me at the airport. He talked to me for the fifteen minutes as we waited for my luggage. I know this is hard to believe, but I absolutely did not understand one thing he said. I know he was speaking English, but what I was hearing was gibberish. At first, I blamed my ears for being plugged by the flight, but after they unclogged, I realized I just could not understand what he was saying. It was a combination of very fast talk coupled with a drawl I have never experienced. I hoped that he was an isolated case while on this hunt. The two-hour trip out to the camp was miserable as I mostly listened and only nodded in agreement. When we got to the camp, which was beyond nice, I met the other guides and the camp staff. Everyone spoke the same. I'm thinking a week of this, and I'll be saying more than once "YOU'VE GOT TO BE KIDDING." The other hunters in the camp were having the same difficulties with the language.

Mount Peyton Lodge

It appeared that in the morning, we would ride four-wheelers with the guide in front and the hunter on the back. I am always excited to begin a hunt but this time more so than the others. I am getting so close to finish of the North American 29 that I want to get going. We were to leave the camp around six thirty, and I was awake very early. There was a clock on the wall at the camp, and it seemed like the time was off a little bit, but I didn't think much of it. We finished breakfast, and I'm dressed and ready to go at six thirty. Everyone else appears ready, and I can't believe we aren't going. The group is standing around, talking about things I can't understand. I wait, and when seven o'clock hits, we depart. I'm confused by the time, but it's possible I heard them wrong when we talked about departure time.

I feel lucky today as we head out in the dark. The trails are incredibly rough, and riding on the back of a four-wheeler is never comfortable. At daybreak, we come to a huge flat area that looks at least ten miles across. Water is interspersed with a few islands of stunted, goofy-looking trees. This is woodland caribou country.

The swamps the caribou call home

We set out on foot, wading through the water. It is about six inches deep and actually easy to walk in as the ground underneath is firm and not the usual mud you find in most watery places.

The first day we travel at least twelve miles around and in the lake. The caribou are nonexistent, but we'll find them tomorrow.

The hiking was very comfortable. I have spent much of the summer getting in shape—again. I have been running five miles four times a week and have lost about 35 pounds. Part of my success was because of the parting of the ways I had with my diet Pepsi. You read earlier that I usually drink a lot of soda, and it had been six weeks since my last one. In the camp, I had a dilemma as the choices for quenching thirst were either water or diet Pepsi. I hate the taste of water, and there was no crystal light or other additives to make it tasty. So after the long hike, I opted for the soda. The taste was incredible, and I now know what smokers experience when they have that first cigarette after a period of abstinence. That would be the last time I stopped drinking soda. I guess I'm doomed to a life of obesity, possibly caused by an addiction to diet soda.

The camp couldn't be any more fun as these guys are constantly pulling stunts on one another. The stunt I pulled in the 9/11 chapter when I hid the caribou horns is a mild example of the goings-on here in the camp. I have never laughed so much. They also were telling jokes, and sometimes I would understand enough to actually get the punch line. My grasp of their talk is getting better.

We were scheduled to leave again at 6:30 a.m. from the camp, and just like yesterday, we leave at 7:00 sharp. I finally ask my guide about the time, and he looks at me funny and begins to laugh. I am really confused now because of his laughter. The look on my face must have set something in motion in his thinking as he says, "I'll bet no one told you about Newfie time." Okay, you're right, I have no idea what Newfie time is. He then tells me that in Newfoundland, the time zone only changes a half hour instead of the usual hour. Therefore, my watch is off by half an hour. I start to laugh myself about my lack of knowledge, but I still have to say to him, "YOU'VE GOT TO BE KIDDING."

Today and day number 3 were more of the same fun, hiking through the swamps. We were in a different area each day, but the overall feature was lots of water. I still have not seen a caribou, but they assure me they do exist. I am not discouraged as I have a great feeling on this hunt. The ride to and from the camp over the incredibly rough trails is taking a toll on my back, but the energy these people put out overshadows the little bit of pain I am experiencing.

On day number 4, we decide to go to a more wooded area, although there is still plenty of water. The sun is actually shining, which is the first time since the hunt began. A short walk produces caribou. My guide says they seem to be a sun-loving species and seem to escape the cover of trees on fall days like today. The herd is about twenty animals with one lone bull. They are quite some distance away, and we plan our strategy, which includes walking around a very large wooded area and getting on the other side of them. The estimated time for this is about an hour, so we hope the sunshine remains. I ask about the noise we are making as we slosh through the water, and this is OK. The bull we are pursuing is not the biggest in the world but is at least average. He appears to have a very large shovel but very short main beams. If the stalk works correctly, we will be able to assess him better as we will be within one hundred yards.

The guide has judged perfectly, and the bull stands at a little over one hundred yards away. He has a beautiful white mane. The bodies of these caribou are larger than their cousins in Alaska or the Northwest Territories. The herd is standing still, which marks the first caribou that I have seen behave this way. Normally, they are constantly moving, and the hunter trying to cut them off for a shot. The decision to take this bull is delayed by the fact that we have time to decide, which is unusual while caribou hunting. The bull looks the same now as our first look at him from afar. His shovel is incredible, but the rest of his horns are just average. I tell the guide that I would be thrilled to have this trophy, and we get ready for a shot. I find a tree and use a branch for a rest, and in one shot from the .300 Weatherby, I have my twenty-eighth species. The shovel turns out to be even larger than we thought and is easily the best one ever taken in Don's camp. I am so happy and thank God for how far he has taken me on my journey.

The picture taking is a little unusual as we are standing in water. After getting to the camp with our load of meat and antlers, we decide it's time to hunt moose. I purchased a tag to hunt them if I got my caribou early. Don allows this, and you pay only a trophy fee if a moose is taken. The moose here are what SCI classifies as Eastern Canadian moose. Technically, if I take a moose here, I would have the North American 29. That would be incredible, but somehow I'm not feeling it. It would appear that God's plan for me is to finish with the polar bear. That hunt is planned for next spring in March. If I don't take a moose here, I also have a Shiras moose hunt in British Columbia immediately after I leave. The Shiras hunt will be the second time I try for it as I was there in British Columbia last fall. The weather had been unusually hot, and I didn't even see a moose in six days. Either moose could finish the twenty-nine species for me.

Number 28 only one to go!

The moose here in Newfoundland occupy different terrain than the caribou. They are in the low mountains and heavier timber. We spent the time mostly traveling the logging trails with the four-wheeler. We did a bit of stopping to glass, but mostly, the guide felt we could see moose moving about in the clear-cuts, so we drove the logging trails. In two days, we saw one cow moose, but I thought that was great as that's more than I had seen in British Columbia.

The moose was not to be on this hunt, but the time pursuing them was a blast as the Newfies are very crazy, fun-loving people. We took time to celebrate the end of the hunt by checking out some of the local hangouts. What's really surprising here is that as most people consume so much alcohol, their speech gets slurred, but in the case of the Newfies, their speech actually got better as they couldn't talk so fast.

I am so pleased overall with this trip and getting my twenty-eighth species. Now it is on to British Columbia to try again for the Shiras. I am not looking forward to the flight as it is six hours from St. John's, Newfoundland, to Vancouver, British Columbia. As you've already seen and read, my patience is very limited, and long airplane rides are almost impossible. The trip from St. John's, Newfoundland, to Vancouver is ridiculously long, and I hated it. I then flew over to the Okanogan Valley to try again for the Shiras moose. The weather was identical to the previous year, and in six days, I couldn't get a glimpse of even one moose. As stated earlier, it appears as though God's plan for me is to finish my journey with a polar bear.

CHAPTER 24

Nanook Final

When we left chapter 1, John, my Inuit guide, was coming down off the pressure ridge with a smile on his face. Being the comedian I know him to be, I am sure he will have some wild tale he is going to tell me. As he approaches the dogs and the wood sled that has been my ride for the past seventeen days, I start to recall how it is that I am here.

I have thought of taking a polar bear for many years. These thoughts escalated since last fall when I got my woodland caribou in Newfoundland, Canada. With that species, I reached the twenty-eighth animal in my quest for the North American 29. I have had this bear hunt booked for nearly five years, and the idea of finishing with a polar bear is so intriguing for me that I really hope John has great news.

The words seem to come in slow motion as I think I hear John say, "Polar bear sleeping." I shake my head in an effort to hear more plainly, and he repeats, "Polar bear sleeping." I just look at his frozen face and his sly little smile. I say, "John, we have been out here seventeen days. We've seen quite a few bears, some close and some far away, and I've listened to many of your funny stories, but this time, I've got to say YOU'VE GOT TO BE KIDDING!" How gullible does he think I am to believe that at this juncture, we are going to find a polar bear asleep out in the middle of the Arctic Ocean? He may have been more believable if he hadn't played so many tricks on me in the past two and a half weeks.

My thoughts go back to many of the hunts where I have successfully taken great trophies. The usual scenario for my success involved what I describe as "paying my dues" before I would take any species. In some cases, I felt I paid more than the normal dues, such as the Alaskan brown bear or the black bear. In both instances, I needed three different hunts to be successful. For the rest of the species, I was very fortunate and only had to hunt one time for each species. I guess most would call me very lucky. I tend to think that I made most of my luck by being ready and able to go where my guide thought we should go. I think it is as important, as I said earlier in the book, that you have complete faith in God and your guide and their decisions. I really think this will swing the good luck pendulum in your favor.

Will I be lucky here at this point in time on this hunt? I feel as though I've paid my bear dues considering the extreme temperatures, the number of days out on the sea ice, and the four-foot-tall "Hilton" we've been calling home. I have prayed since this hunt began for God to keep us safe, and yes, I've also prayed that I be successful at finishing my goal. Is this selfish on my part? God always grants your wishes even though you may question His decisions at the time. I am optimistic in my thinking that I haven't asked God for more than I deserve.

Okay, John is now waving for me to get out of the sled and follow him back up the icy trail to the top of the pressure ridge. I humor him and actually follow. This ridge is taller than most at about thirty feet high, and I have a hard time climbing it. My boots are made for operating on a flat surface, but after a few slips and falls, I actually get to the top. John points, and I look through my binoculars that he has handed back to me, and I see a slightly yellow spot out on the sea ice. Now this is surreal as there really is a polar bear sleeping out on the sea ice. He appears to be sleeping next to an airhole the seals are keeping open for breathing. I feel so bad for not believing John, but you know it really is irrelevant now. I estimate the yardage at over 500 yards. The bear is too far for a shot, and I turn to seek advice from John. He is already down off the ridge and waving for me to do the same. Down I go with a little less effort than the trip up. John, in his quiet demeanor, says our plan will be to get back in the dogsled and try to find an area to cross to the opposite side of the ridge. Then if we can find a place to actually cross, we will then take off after the

The ice is so blue in the pressure ridges

bear and hope we can sneak up on him or at least get him running and tire him out enough to let some of the dogs loose and put him at bay. My first question to John is "How do you know it's a male?" John answers by saying "He is a male!" I guess that's an answer, maybe just a little short on explanation.

I think over the options and ask John about the best estimate of distance to find somewhere to get across the pressure ridge. He really has no idea, and I recall other times in the past when we crossed ridges. This has been no easy task as they can go on for miles with no possible way to cross. All I can say is "YOU'VE GOT TO BE KIDDING." If we can cross the ridge, the problem then becomes the dogs. They are always barking so I have no idea how you would sneak up on a sleeping bear. I wanted this bear so badly that I really didn't think the plan John was offering would work. This thinking goes against what I just said a few paragraphs earlier, but the one thing I've seen is bears in general like to wonder and don't hold in one place very long.

I look at John and offer an idea. I say, "What would happen if I try to walk after the bear? The wind is in our favor, the bear is sleeping, and I am capable of taking a fairly long shot." I can see the questionable look on his face, but it seems I have gained his confidence. He says he will stay with the dogs and watch my progress. We can always go back to his plan if needed.

The climb to the top of the ridge this time is even harder as now I have my rifle and pack. On the other side, I begin the walk to the bear. I am already soaked with sweat as my sixty-below-zero clothing was made to keep me warm but not for extended physical activity. My thoughts go from *Will I be ready to take a shot?* to *How close will I get before he awakens?* The anticipation is excruciating. Then I begin to think that I don't know how big this bear is, although he looks like quite a pile of hair as he lies on the ground. The next thought is if he really is a male. I don't want to take a female as one of goals for the North American 29 is for them to all be males. Next, I wonder if my rifle will work. I have read so many stories about hunters who went to take a shot in these extreme temperatures and the firing pin was frozen. For this hunt, just as in preparation for my muskox hunt, I took my .300 Weatherby to the local gunsmith and had him totally clean all the oil and grease from the firing mechanisms. It worked fine for the muskox, so it should work now. *All right,* I think, *enough with the pessimistic thinking!*

I continue walking at a slow pace as to not to be completely overheated. I need to have faith that John is right. This is a male, and he is better than an average bear. The equipment will work, and I will shoot perfectly. The moment of truth arrives as I approach the 250-yard mark. The bear appears to awaken as I see a seal poke his head out of the sea ice from the hole next to the bear. It is gone immediately, making a mockery of the bear. Now he is awake and starts to get to his feet. He hasn't seen me, and I get ready for my chance at finishing my dream. I am so nervous I can't stop shaking. I have to settle down, or this bear will soon be on the move.

He shakes the sleepiness from his body and moves around the hole as if expecting to catch dinner. As he turns and quarters away from me, I drop to the ground and throw my backpack down. I quickly get the rifle on the makeshift rest I have made with my backpack and fire a shot. The bear goes down immediately. I eject the spent shell and wait for movement. He is down for good, and now I can't move. I just lie there, not really believing what has just happened.

Barking dogs is the next sound I hear. John is on his way to me with the sled. I'm not sure how long I've been in a daze, but evidently, John found a way to cross the ridge with the dogs and sled. I am now up and screaming at the top of my lungs. "I got him!" Then I'm back to the ground, and I do a snow angel while continuing to yell "This is unbelievable!" On my knees, I continue to tell the world, "I have finished my North American 29!" Obviously, my screams fail to excite any eardrums, but I don't care, and the screaming continues. "Thank you, God, for getting me through!"

The happiest hunter in the world

John is only off the sled for a second before I bowl him over with a huge hug. He appears as excited as I am. We rise and continue with high fives and more screaming. I am ecstatic. What an incredible feeling! You've always heard of someone having a huge weight lifted from his shoulders. Well, this is the feeling I'm enjoying. My joy continues, but now I am in tears. I'm thinking of all the years of planning, the time away from Becky and the kids, and the incredible beauty I've experienced. It's ridiculous that I'm crying, and I try to contain my feelings, but it's impossible. I say to John to give me a few more minutes to sob and pray, and I'll be ready to go to the bear.

John the "jokester" and I

Any time a hunter approaches his fallen prey, there is always a moment of total respect for the animal. Of course, you want to immediately know the trophy size, but before that, thoughts occur, such as where they live and what transpired to bring you to this point in time. I have such respect for all the big game species. The old males lead a very hard life. If they survive the rut each year, after losing up to 30 percent of their body weight, the winters can be killers for them. Most animals by the time they reach trophy status have very short lives from that point on. I guess that there is a natural bond between older hunters and older animals, both having experienced a long and fulfilling life.

The bear I have taken is an old male, making John look incredibly smart. He is perfect in every way. There is not a hair missing on his coat of beautiful white hollow hairs, and he is not all beat up from fighting with other males during the rut. He is in a great position for pictures, and I take more pictures of this bear than I sometimes took of two or three species combined. I am so proud of what I have accomplished. I want all the memories I can retain with the pictures I am taking. John couldn't be any happier for me. I don't think he has guided someone who completed his or her North American 29.

Tea anyone?

Just as we are about to leave with the bear hide and the meat John wants for his family, he springs another of his tricks on me. He says it's the Inuit custom to eat the liver of a fallen bear. I look at him, and this time I can't tell if he is joking or not; after all, I have been proven wrong with the sleeping bear story. He smiles that same wily smile, and I say, "YOU'VE GOT TO BE KIDDING." He's not kidding, and we proceed to eat the bear's liver. I don't know to this day how in the world I ate it, but we did indeed partake of raw, fresh, warm polar bear liver. I have no idea if this really is a local custom or not. When I returned to Holman and I inquired about the custom, I got the same wily smile from all of them as John had given me.

We returned to the tent before nightfall. My sleep was

uninterrupted that night as it was a little warmer, and I didn't have to worry about our plan for tomorrow. I was refreshed as we packed up for the trip back to Holman. This would be a journey of over two days with the dogs and then the snowmobiles, but I was okay. The temperature was at least livable at -30 degrees, and the sun was shining. It would be a glorious ride back in my old wood sled, and I would have many hours to reminisce about all the hunting trips of the past twenty years. I was happy. I couldn't wait to get to a telephone to give Becky the incredible news. I know she will be as thrilled as I am, although her reasons may be just a little different.

We arrived back in the middle of the afternoon, and as you read in chapter 1, I checked into the remaining room of two rooms at the Holman hotel. Wisconsin Jim had the other room. The wait would be three days until the plane arrived from Yellowknife to take us home. I visited with the locals and met most of the residents, and they are wonderful, caring people. They are all fun-loving but most of their stories I always questioned. I had another chance to see the farthest north golf course in North America. As I mentioned earlier, I will never complain about golf course conditions after seeing this rocky place.

The two room hotel

When I thought about it, how could I complain about anything as God has blessed my life so many times? I have now added to my list of great achievements in life with the accomplishment of taking the North American 29. I have taken all twenty-nine with my .300 Weatherby rifle. Don Behrns mounted all twenty-nine species for me. I have been a national president for the U.S. Custom Harvesters. I have owned and operated, along with my brothers Herb and Steve, one of the largest custom harvest operations in the United States. I have been a very large farmer, probably in the top 10 percent of all farms in size of acres in the United States. The latest accomplishment is writing down my memoirs of hunting with these pages. However, most of all, I have a loving wife of thirty-two years, three wonderful children, a great family, and many friends. How could it get any better?

CHAPTER 25

What's Next?

Becky and I built a new home in Gilbert, Arizona, in late 2005. This would serve as our winter retreat from the harsh conditions of South Dakota. The house was big enough to facilitate the moving of my North American 29 collection from the farm in South Dakota to Arizona. We did exactly that in the winter of 2006 to 2007. I was allowed the entryway, one side room on the main floor and one room on the second floor to display my life's passion. It seemed incredible that the space could hold over thirty-five works of taxidermy, especially considering fourteen of them were full-body mounts. The house was full, but we did a great job of arranging the mounts. The public interest in the collection was overwhelming. The visitors, many of whom were strangers, showed up at our home to view the animals and hear my hunting stories. The groups, some large and others small, consisted mostly of people who had learned of my collection through word of mouth. During the winter months, we would have groups ringing the doorbell up to three times a week. I couldn't have been more pleased as I loved the attention my collection was getting. A common question was if I was still hunting. I gave them this answer: "Becky says I am like the federal government in that I am way over budget!"

One night Becky and I talked about doing something to display the collection to the public. A few years back, we had discussed a restaurant using a hunting theme. The planned site at that time was Mitchell, South Dakota. Now as we talked, the idea of a restaurant close to home in Gilbert started to make some sense. My good friend Dan says to me all the time that I'm not happy unless I have a major

239

project going. He may be right. In the spring of 2008, our son Brett showed some real interest in getting involved with the new venture. During the summer months, Brett put together a business plan and conducted research for a new restaurant. One of the facts he gathered showed over six hundred thousand hunting license applications in Arizona. That is a huge number. It looked as though there were more than enough hunters to support a hunting-themed restaurant. The business plan showed the people in the local area had incomes that averaged almost $79,000, which would be high enough to support a mid- to high-end steakhouse. With this knowledge, we signed a lease on September 1, 2008, for our new business, aptly named Trophy's Steakhouse. In January, our son Kiel and his wife, Stephanie, moved to Arizona to help us plan, build, and manage Trophy's. They proved a great asset when Becky and I had to be home in South Dakota farming.

Trophy's was an incredible project. We broke ground on January 3, 2009, and on April 7, 2009, we were open for business. Three months is a very short time to do a build-out. The theme is the North American 29. Can you imagine why we chose that? There are other restaurants with a hunting theme, but Trophy's is one of a kind. Becky and I did all the design work; thus, it turned out to be a very comfortable place. Our family worked as we did the painting, some woodwork, plumbing, electrical, and cleaning. Our nephew Jason also helped to build, and then he managed the front of the house after we opened. Our start was slower than we anticipated, but our spirit couldn't be broken. The first summer was slow, except for Father's Day weekend, where we were covered up. We weren't prepared for this. A few weeks earlier, Fox TV on Channel 10 in Phoenix came to the restaurant and filmed a short story on our unique theme and wild game selections on the menu. This probably did more damage than good for our new business. We couldn't handle all the traffic it generated. We survived and moved into our first winter. The traffic picked up 50 percent compared to the summer, so we were excited.

As the first-year anniversary approached, we planned a great party because we had made it a whole year. Statistics show 50 percent of new restaurants fail in the first year. We had made it a year in the worst economic times our country has seen in a long time. Again, we kept our chins up and vowed to have the best customer service and great food. We were a "meat and potatoes" kind of place, and we wanted to move a bit higher on the ratings scale. We started with two stars in the *Arizona Republic* newspaper, and I thanked the very nice lady who did the review for giving us two stars. The important websites rated us at two stars also. We thought we should be thankful we weren't rated zero as we were farmers trying to compete in the highly competitive food service industry. We changed the menu quite a few times, and we now have a pretty nice selection for everyone.

Our craft beer selection is the best in the East Gilbert and Queen Creek area. We have come a long way. As we approach our three-year anniversary, our sales based on a month-to-month comparison to the previous year have shown 20 percent to 25 percent growth. Our rating on Yelp is now four out of five. That isn't too bad for a new restaurant in the Phoenix area, operating in a terrible recession and a theme that is not necessarily to the liking of everyone.

For our next project, we have been looking at building a sports bar, which will include a microbrewery. Who knows? There may be another book about some of the experiences with our restaurant customers. The title would be *I Can't Make This Stuff Up!* Or maybe Becky and I will actually retire.

Trophy's Steakhouse is a one of a kind!

The private room

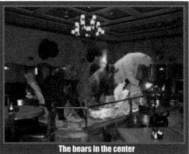
The bears in the center

Grand slam as the back bar

Looking down the side at the booths

Elk and the fireplace

APPENDIX 1

The following table represents the chronological order of my pursuit of the "North American 29." I accomplished my collection in just sixteen years. The table shows, as previously written, how fortunate I was on most of my hunts. I met my overall goals as every animal is a male of the species and they all qualified for the SCI record book. An interesting note is the years when I didn't hunt anywhere meant the hunting fund was very low!

MY NORTH AMERICAN 29

Number	ANIMAL/SPECIES	LOCATION TAKEN	DATE
29	Polar Bear	Beaufort Sea, Northwest Territories, Canada	4/1/2007
28	Woodland Caribou	Gander, Newfoundland, Canada	10/1/2006
27	Common Grizzly Bear	Chetwyn, British Columbia, Canada	6/15/2006
26	Mountain lion	Tusuyan, Arizona	2/3/2006
25	Columbia Black Tail Deer	Medford, Oregon	11/1/2005
24	Coastal (Pacific) Black Bear	Queen Charlotte Islands, British Columbia, Canada	10/12/2005
23	Roosevelt Elk	Santa Rosa Island, California	9/2/2005
22	American Bison	Northern Saskatchewan, Canada	10/13/2004
21	Central Canadian Barren Ground Caribou	Little Martin Lake, Northwest Territories, Canada	9/7/2004
20	Continental (Inland) Bear	Beluga Mountain, Alaska	8/12/2004

19	Alaska Brown Bear	Stopovak Bay, Alaska Peninsula, Alaska	5/14/2004
18	Quebec Labrador Caribou	Whale River, Quebec, Canada	9/5/2002
17	Greenland Musk ox	Holman Island, Northwest Territories, Canada	3/2/2002
16	Western Canada Moose	Ganado River, British Columbia, Canada	8/30/2000
15	American Mountain Goat	Muncho Lake, British Columbia, Canada	9/5/2000
14	Mountain Caribou	Muncho Lake, British Columbia, Canada	9/7/2000
13	Desert Mule Deer	Hermisillo, Sonora, Mexico	1/8/1999
12	Desert Bighorn Sheep	Los Mochas Mountains, Sonora, Mexico	2/23/1997
11	Coues' Whitetail Deer	Hermisillo, Sonora, Mexico	12/12/1996
10	Northwestern Whitetail Deer	Fort Vermillion, Alberta, Canada	11/22/1996
9	Gray Wolf	Yakutat, Alaska	9/2/1995
8	Rocky Mountain Bighorn Sheep	Wilmore Wilderness, Alberta, Canada	10/7/1994
7	Stone Sheep	Scoop Lake, British Columbia, Canada	8/25/1993
6	Rocky Mountain Mule Deer	Gillette, Wyoming	10/19/1992
5	Pronghorn	Gillette, Wyoming	10/18/1992
4	Alaskan-Yukon Moose	Canning River, Brooks Range, Alaska	9/2/1992
3	Alaskan-Yukon Barren Ground Caribou	Brooks Range, Alaska	8/27/1992
2	Dall Sheep	Brooks Range, Alaska	8/1/1992
1	Rocky Mountain Elk	Steamboat Springs, Colorado	10/21/1991